IEG

Independent Evaluation of IFC's Development Results 2007

Lessons and Implications from 10 Years of Experience

D1305552

http://www.ifc.org/ieg

2007
Washington, D.C.

IFC
International
Finance
Corporation
World Bank Group

Photo: Teamwork on a construction site in Cairo, Egypt. Photograph by Amal Zarif Labib.

ISBN: 978-0-8213-7264-7
e-ISBN: 978-0-8213-7265-4
DOI: 10.1596/978-0-8213-7264-7

Library of Congress Cataloging-in-Publication Data have been applied for.

World Bank InfoShop
E-mail: pic@worldbank.org
Telephone: 202-458-4500
Facsimile: 202-522-1500

Independent Evaluation Group–IFC
E-mail: AskIEG@ifc.org
Telephone: 202-458-2299
Facsimile: 202-974-4302

 Printed on Recycled Paper

Contents

Tables

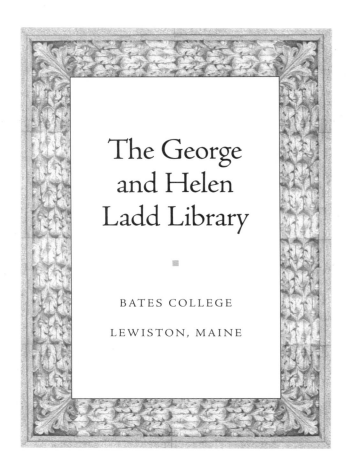

The George and Helen Ladd Library

■

BATES COLLEGE

LEWISTON, MAINE

ABBREVIATIONS

CAS	Country Assistance Strategy
DOTS	Development Outcome Tracking System
EBRD	European Bank for Reconstruction and Development
FI	Financial intermediary
FY	Fiscal year
GDP	Gross domestic product
IEG	Independent Evaluation Group
IFC	International Finance Corporation
MIC	Middle-income country
PSD	Private sector development
SME	Small and medium enterprise
XPSR	Expanded Project Supervision Report

Acknowledgments

This report was prepared by a team led by Dan Crabtree and Hiroyuki Hatashima, drawing upon research and contributions from Susan Chaffin, Jouni Eerikainen, Nisachol Mekharat, Maria Elena Pinglo, Stephen Pirozzi, Miguel Angel Rebolledo, Cherian Samuel, and Victoria Viray-Mendoza. Yvette Jarencio, Marylou Kam-Cheong, and Rosemarie Pena provided general administrative support to the study team. Helen Chin edited the report; and Sid Edelmann, Sona Panajyan, and Vivian Jackson managed its production and dissemination.

The evaluation was written with the guidance of Nicholas Burke, Head of Micro Evaluation, IEG-IFC; and Linda Morra-Imas, Head of Macro Evaluation, IEG-IFC, and under the overall leadership of Marvin Taylor-Dormond, Director, IEG-IFC.

The report benefited substantially from the constructive advice and feedback from many staff at IFC, and also from a number of Independent Evaluation Group (IEG) colleagues in both IFC and in the World Bank. Peer review was provided by Nils Fostvedt (IEG-Bank) and David McKenzie (Development Research Group, World Bank).

Director-General, Evaluation, World Bank Group
Vinod Thomas

Director, IEG-IFC	*Marvin Taylor-Dormond*
Acting Manager	*Denis Carpio*
Head of Macro Evaluation	*Linda Morra-Imas*
Head of Micro Evaluation	*Nicholas Burke*
Head, Communication, Knowledge and Quality	*Sidney Edelmann*
Task Managers	*Dan Crabtree*
	Hiroyuki Hatashima
Study Team	
Senior Environmental Specialist	*Jouni Eerikainen*
Senior Evaluation Officer	*Stephen Pirozzi*
Senior Evaluation Officer	*Miguel Angel Rebolledo*
Evaluation Officer	*Cherian Samuel*
Evaluation Analyst	*Nisachol Mekharat*
Evaluation Analyst	*Maria Elena Pinglo*
Evaluation Analyst	*Victoria Viray-Mendoza*

Foreword

As part of the World Bank Group, IFC's overriding objective is to help reduce poverty and support sustainable development in developing countries. IFC pursues this mission by supporting the private sector to create jobs and stimulate markets. This report, which assesses the impact of IFC toward that mission, appears at a time of unprecedented levels of private investment in the emerging markets.

The report takes a look back at the development results that IFC-supported projects have achieved in the last 10 years, the main lessons that have emerged at the project level, and the strategic implications for IFC going forward, in the context of rapid organizational growth.

In the last decade, 59 percent of IFC-supported projects (65 percent by volume) achieved high development ratings. In addition, profitability and development impact have tended to go together, with about half of projects delivering high development results and acceptable IFC returns, and about one-third of projects achieving low development rating and a less than acceptable IFC return. These results are expected to be sustained for projects to be evaluated in 2007 and 2008, due to improved project risk layering by IFC at approval and reduced business climate risk in many client countries since project approval (in 2002 and 2003, respectively).

The report finds that IFC-supported project performance is closely linked to the quality of a country's business climate, the presence of a high-quality sponsor, well-managed company and product market risk, and in particular, to IFC's work quality (especially at the appraisal and structuring stage, and including oversight of the environmental and social effects of projects). There are also several other factors that improve IFC's quality of development impact: IFC's ability to offer local currency financing, its reach to small and medium enterprises through financial intermediaries, and the nature of linkages between its investment and advisory services.

Going forward, the report highlights major challenges IFC faces to achieving overall development effectiveness. IFC will need to adopt a sharper country focus and better exploit synergies with the Bank and other development partners in improving business climates in developing countries. Furthermore, rapid and increasingly decentralized growth will need to be managed carefully to ensure high work quality. Finally, risk-management systems and risk-mitigation products will have to continue to evolve to help IFC prepare and deliver improved services to clients.

Vinod Thomas
Director-General, Evaluation

Avant-propos

En tant qu'institution du Groupe de la Banque mondiale, la Société financière internationale (IFC) a avant tout pour objectif de promouvoir la réduction de la pauvreté et de favoriser un développement durable dans les pays en développement. Elle s'acquitte de cette mission en aidant le secteur privé à créer des emplois et à stimuler les marchés. Ce rapport, qui évalue la contribution de l'IFC à cette mission, paraît à un moment où l'investissement privé sur les marchés émergents atteint des niveaux sans précédent.

Le rapport fait le bilan des accomplissements des projets financés par l'IFC au cours des dix dernières années au plan du développement, reprend les principales leçons qui se dégagent au niveau des projets et analyse leurs implications pour la stratégie future de la Société dans le contexte de la croissance rapide de l'organisation.

Au cours des dix dernières années, 59 % des projets soutenus par l'IFC (65 % en volume) ont obtenu des notes élevées pour leur impact sur le développement. Rentabilité et impact sur le développement vont, par ailleurs, généralement de pair : la moitié environ des projets affichent de bons résultats en termes de développement et un taux de rentabilité acceptable pour l'IFC, et environ un tiers des projets obtiennent une note médiocre en termes de développement et un taux de rentabilité moins qu'acceptable pour l'IFC. Il devrait en être de même pour les projets dont l'évaluation est prévue en 2007 et en 2008 par suite

d'une meilleure segmentation des risques liés aux projets par l'IFC au moment de l'approbation et de la réduction des risques liés au climat des affaires dans de nombreux pays clients après l'approbation des projets (respectivement en 2002 et en 2003).

Le rapport conclut que la performance des projets financés par l'IFC est étroitement liée à la qualité du climat des affaires dans un pays, à la présence d'une solide entité parrainante, à la bonne gestion de l'entreprise, à la maîtrise du risque de marché et, en particulier, à la qualité des interventions de l'IFC (notamment au stade de l'évaluation et de la structuration, et durant la supervision de l'impact environnemental et social des projets). Plusieurs autres facteurs améliorent la qualité de l'impact des interventions de l'IFC au plan du développement : la possibilité qu'elle a de proposer des financements en monnaie nationale et de faire profiter les petites et moyennes entreprises de son action par le biais d'intermédiaires financiers, et la nature des liens existant entre ses opérations d'investissement et ses services-conseil.

Le rapport expose les difficultés majeures que rencontrera l'IFC à l'avenir pour assurer l'efficacité générale de son action de développement. La Société devra axer davantage ses interventions sur chaque pays et mieux exploiter les synergies avec la Banque et les autres partenaires de développement pour améliorer le climat des affaires dans le monde en développement. Elle devra aussi gérer avec soin la rapide expansion et décentralisation de ses activités pour en assurer la qualité. Enfin, il importera que les systèmes de gestion et les produits d'atténuation des risques continuent d'évoluer pour lui permettre de concevoir et de fournir de meilleures prestations à ses clients.

Vinod Thomas
Directeur général, Évaluation

Prólogo

Como parte del Grupo del Banco Mundial, el objetivo principal de la Corporación Financiera Internacional (IFC, por su sigla en inglés) es ayudar a reducir la pobreza y apoyar el desarrollo sostenible en países en desarrollo. La IFC trata de cumplir este objetivo brindando apoyo al sector privado, a fin de crear puestos de trabajo y estimular a los mercados. Este informe, en el que se evalúa el impacto de la IFC en el contexto de esa misión, se publica en un momento en el que la inversión privada registra niveles sin precedentes en mercados emergentes.

El informe contempla los resultados de desarrollo que han logrado los proyectos respaldados por la IFC en los últimos 10 años, las principales lecciones que se obtuvieron a nivel de los proyectos y las consecuencias estratégicas a futuro para la Corporación, en el contexto de un rápido crecimiento institucional.

En la última década, el 59% de los proyectos respaldados por la IFC (un 65% en términos de volumen) logró altas calificaciones de desarrollo. Además, el impacto sobre el desarrollo y la rentabilidad han tendido a producirse en forma conjunta: cerca de la mitad de los proyectos generó resultados altos en términos de desarrollo y retornos aceptables para la IFC, mientras que un tercio de los proyectos alcanzó una baja calificación de desarrollo y retornos para la IFC por debajo de lo aceptable. Se espera que estos resultados se mantengan en los proyectos a evaluar en 2007 y 2008, gracias una mejora en la estructuración de

riesgo del proyecto por parte de la IFC al momento de la aprobación y una reducción del riesgo del ambiente para los negocios en muchos países clientes desde la aprobación de los proyectos (en 2002 y 2003, respectivamente).

El informe concluye que el desempeño de los proyectos respaldados por la IFC está íntimamente relacionado con la calidad del ambiente para los negocios de un país, con la presencia de un patrocinador de calidad, con una buena gestión del riesgo de empresas y del mercado de productos y, en especial, con la calidad del trabajo de la IFC (especialmente en la etapa de evaluación y estructuración, y también en la supervisión de los impactos ambientales y sociales de los proyectos). Existen muchos otros factores que mejoran la calidad del impacto de la IFC en términos de desarrollo: la capacidad de la IFC para ofrecer financiamiento en moneda nacional, su alcance a pequeñas y medianas empresas a través de intermediarios financieros y el carácter de la integración entre sus servicios de inversión y asesoría.

A futuro, el informe destaca algunos importantes desafíos que enfrenta la IFC al momento de lograr eficacia en términos de desarrollo general. La IFC tendrá que adoptar un enfoque más específico para cada país y aprovechar de mejor manera las sinergias con el Banco y otros socios de desarrollo, a fin de mejorar el ambiente para los negocios en los países en desarrollo. Además, será preciso gestionar cuidadosamente el crecimiento rápido y cada vez más descentralizado si se pretende garantizar la calidad del trabajo. Por último, es necesario que los sistemas de gestión de riesgo y los productos de mitigación de riesgo sigan evolucionando para que la IFC pueda preparar y prestar mejores servicios a los clientes.

Vinod Thomas
Director General, Evaluación

Executive Summary

This is the tenth annual review by the Independent Evaluation Group of the International Financial Corporation (IEG-IFC).[1] In each review, IEG assesses IFC's performance in promoting sustainable private sector development in all developing countries. The 2007 review affords IEG the opportunity to look back at a decade of results for IFC's private sector operations, and to ask

- Have IFC-supported projects achieved sound development results—financially, economically, environmentally, and socially?
- What has been learned about private sector development after 10 years of evaluation?
- What are the strategic implications for IFC in improving its development performance in the next few years?

Development Results of IFC-Supported Projects, 1996–2006

IFC's development role is clearly mandated in its Articles of Agreement and Mission Statement. Article 1 states that IFC will "seek to stimulate, and to help create conditions conducive to the flow of private capital, domestic and foreign, into productive investment in member countries." In seeking to deliver development impact, IFC pursues a fourfold mission: to promote open and competitive markets, to support companies and other private sector partners, to generate productive jobs and deliver basic services, and to create opportunities for people to escape poverty and improve their lives. IFC uses two types of development intervention: financial products and advisory services.

Since 1991, IFC has increased its financial activities approximately sixfold, investing approximately $50 billion in developing countries through its loan and equity operations. Including funds provided by cofinanciers, IFC-supported projects have consistently made up about 4 percent of all private capital flows to developing countries. IFC investments are more than twice as concentrated as foreign direct investment in what the institution considers to be *frontier* countries—defined as low-income by the World Bank, and/or high risk.[2] IFC investments also account for about 30 percent of International Finance Institution private sector volumes. The World Bank provided approximately $340 billion of assistance to the governments of developing countries during this time, with much more static, year-on-year volume changes than those of IFC.

Majority of Evaluated Projects Achieved High Development Ratings

Out of 627 investment operations approved during 1991–2001, and evaluated between 1996 and 2006 (as the projects reached operating maturity),[3] 59 percent (65 percent by volume) achieved high development ratings at the project level. That is, most projects were, on balance, delivering (and were expected to deliver in the long run) sustainable results—across indicators measuring their financial, economic, environmental, and social performance—as well as contributing to private sector development generally. These results in part reflect the market test that IFC projects face, meaning they cannot be compared directly with those of public-sector-oriented development institutions such as the World Bank.[4] Performance has varied significantly by sector and by region, with the results of IFC-supported projects in Africa lagging those in other regions, mainly due to the more challenging business climates and weaker environmental and social compliance among IFC's clients.

Profitability and Development Impact Usually Go Hand-in-Hand

In addition to evaluating the development results of IFC-supported projects, IEG also examines whether its investment operations contribute positively to IFC's own profitability (and thus its ability to fund its future operations from retained earnings). To achieve a high investment return rating, a loan must be expected to be repaid as scheduled, while an equity investment should provide IFC with a return above that of a loan, commensurate with the extra instrument risk. Although fewer equity investments are judged successful on this basis (31 percent had above-benchmark returns, compared with 74 percent for loans), those that are deemed so contribute to high overall portfolio returns for IFC.

When the investment results of IFC operations are considered alongside project development results, about a half of IFC projects evaluated during 1996–2006 had *high-high* ratings (high development ratings at the project level and an acceptable IFC investment return from the operation) while about a third had *low-low* ratings

(low development results; less than acceptable IFC investment return). This shows that IFC has not actively supported projects where there was a trade-off between development results and investment returns. Projects fail to achieve *high-high* ratings for a number of reasons, including the inherent commercial risk in different industry sectors, adverse business climates, poor sponsor quality, or shortfalls in IFC's work quality.

Comprehensive Assessment of IFC's Development Effectiveness Is Challenging

IFC is making significant improvements in how it measures development performance at the project level, but methodological challenges remain before IFC can fully identify its overall development effectiveness at the sector, country, regional and global levels. IFC's monitoring and self-evaluation systems have advanced such that IFC is starting to measure its development results across its portfolio of investment and advisory operations (primarily through a Development Outcome Tracking System introduced in 2005). Building on that progress, these systems will need to evolve to capture the wider sector and country impacts of the projects that IFC supports.

There has been gradual progress toward harmonizing the private sector evaluation standards of multilateral development institutions. While this has resulted in an agreed set of good practice standards, with which IFC is largely compliant, comparing IFC's performance against those of other private sector international finance institutions remains challenging—not least because of varying institutional mandates and objectives.

Lessons from 10 Years of Private Sector Development Evaluation

Five Factors Have Driven Project Performance

There is no magic formula guaranteed to deliver sustainable private sector development across all IFC operations. Nonetheless, after 10 years of evaluation, five factors are seen to significantly influence IFC's development performance at the project level:

- Changes in the quality of a country's business climate following project approval;
- Type of industry sector in which an investment is made;
- Quality of the sponsor;
- Level of product market, client company, and project type risks; and
- IFC work quality.

The extent to which IFC is able to offer local currency options, whether it offers financing directly or indirectly to small and medium enterprises, and the nature of the linkages between advisory services and investment activities also have important consequences for private sector development.

IFC Work Quality Has Been Most Important

The quality of IFC's own project execution and supervision (particularly of environmental and social effects) has been the most critical influence on the development results of IFC-supported projects. This is especially so in Africa, where IFC has, in certain cases, mitigated very high business climate risk through high-quality due diligence and appropriate project structuring. However, IFC's work quality in Africa has generally lagged behind other regions (work quality was rated high in 45 percent of operations in Africa, compared with 68 percent of operations in other regions), highlighting the greater risks that IFC was willing to take historically in the region, as well as challenges in recruiting and retaining suitably experienced staff.

Strategic Implications for IFC

IFC Has Made Sound Strategic Choices Overall but Challenges Remain

Evaluation findings from the past decade broadly support IFC's core directions and priorities. Operations in strategic frontier countries and sectors have generally yielded above-average development results, and IFC has improved its balancing of project risks at approval and its quality of project supervision overall. At the same time, evaluation findings also point to potential areas of risk and of opportunities for IFC in the context of the challenges it set for itself in its 2006 *Strategic Directions* paper.[5] These include greater develop-

ment impact, improved World Bank Group cooperation, leadership in standard setting, improved client satisfaction, sound finances, and a strong staff.

IFC Must Develop a Sharper Country Focus, Especially in Middle-Income Countries

IFC has successfully mobilized funding from a variety of sources to support operations in high-risk and low-income countries in pursuit of its frontier strategy. IFC could now seek to define more sharply its role and priorities in nonfrontier middle-income countries (MICs),[6] where approximately one-third of all people who subsist on less than $2 a day live, and where IFC carries out most of its investment operations. Lack of capacity in domestic financial markets means that many MICs are like low-income countries in having limited or zero availability of long-term, local currency finance, as a result of which exposure to devaluation risk is a widespread problem for enterprises forced to borrow in foreign currency. Infrastructure to support production and trade is another challenge in many MICs, as is tackling large pockets of rural poverty. A valuable role for IFC therefore still exists in many MICs. However, IFC has achieved very weak development results when it has supported projects in which its additionality in MICs was not clear, emphasizing the need for IFC to understand clearly the private sector development dynamics in a country and to identify where its comparative advantage lies so that it can effectively complement existing capital flows.

New Incentives and Mechanisms for World Bank Group Cooperation Are Needed

A stronger country focus could complement IFC's sector and regional efforts, in part by helping to identify opportunities for enhanced cooperation with the World Bank[7] in areas of synergy such as business climate improvement, deepening of financial sector capacity, infrastructure development and environmental and social impact. Cooperation in these areas has brought development gains in counties as diverse as Mexico, the Philippines, and Senegal, and is of utmost importance in Africa, which has fallen far behind other developing markets. In practice, cooperation between IFC and the World Bank in areas of synergy has not reached the level envisaged in Country Assistance Strategies (CASs), and evaluation has uncovered as many inhibitors as facilitators of cooperation. CASs have seldom provided a good framework for cooperation, and new incentives and mechanisms to complement the CAS would be desirable.

IFC Must Ensure Sound Work Quality as It Decentralizes

IFC's current strategy seeks greater development impact through a scaling up of investment and advisory services operations, and stronger local representation through further decentralization of IFC operations. IFC will need to be fully cognizant of the possible trade-offs among rapid growth, organizational change, and project execution quality. During a previous period of significant organizational change in 1998–2001, supervision quality fell sharply. Effectively retaining staff and knowledge are already areas needing attention and such challenges are amplified with further decentralization. IFC might learn from the World Bank's experiences with knowledge management under highly decentralized structures.

Continued Strengthening of Risk Mitigation Required

Experience highlights how markets can quickly withdraw financial support for companies in response to adverse economic or political events. Despite the current investment optimism among investors in much of the developing world, IFC could explicitly address in its strategy the threat of a global investment decline, its likely impact on clients, and any mitigating actions that would be necessary. Planning now to improve risk-management systems, and developing new risk-mitigating products to soften the impact for clients, would strengthen IFC's ability to respond to future economic shocks as well as enhance its countercyclical role.

Recommendations

In seeking to address the many challenges that the IFC faces, IFC Management will need to pursue the following recommendations (see chapter 4 for further details):

- From a client and stakeholder perspective,
  (i) Adopt more tailored country strategies, to complement its strong sector and regional approach, including through the development and pursuit of a set of country-specific private sector development indicators.
  (ii) In its country strategies, flag opportunities to work on the nexus of rural poverty and sustainable natural resources, on which poor people depend, and to identify and develop high-impact agribusiness and rural microfinance projects with widespread demonstration effects, while at the same time providing leadership for promoting socially and environmentally sustainable practices.
- From an internal process perspective, enhance cooperation with the World Bank in areas of synergy,
  (i) By considering, with the Bank, new incentives and mechanisms for cooperation to complement the CAS process.
  (ii) By identifying investments at approval that were facilitated by Bank policy or regulatory assistance to a government, and tracking them throughout the project cycle (through IFC's Development Outcome Tracking System or other means) to judge their success.
- From a human capital perspective, monitor the decentralization process closely to ensure that IFC work quality remains robust and is supported by a rigorous training program for new investment staff.
- From a financial and measurement perspective,
  (i) Make continued efforts to improve its risk-management systems and to prepare for the next correction in the international markets, including perhaps the extended use and development of new risk-mitigation products.
  (ii) With IEG's support, advance its metrics to understand better (and derive lessons about) the wider sector and country-level impacts of the projects that IFC supports.

Résumé analytique

Cet examen est le dixième effectué sur une base annuelle par le Groupe indépendant d'évaluation de la Société financière internationale (IEG-IFC)[1]. Dans le cadre de chaque examen, l'IEG évalue la mesure dans laquelle l'IFC a réussi à promouvoir un développement durable du secteur privé dans tous les pays en développement. L'examen 2007 a été l'occasion pour le Groupe de faire le point des résultats des opérations menées par l'IFC dans le cadre du secteur privé au cours des dix dernières années pour tenter de répondre aux question suivantes :

- Les projets soutenus par l'IFC ont-ils abouti à de bons résultats en matière de développement — aux plans financier, économique, environnemental et social ?
- Quels enseignements peut-on tirer des évaluations réalisées au cours des dix dernières années pour le développement du secteur privé ?
- L'amélioration de l'impact de l'IFC sur le développement au cours des prochaines années a-t-elle des implications stratégiques ?

Résultats au plan du développement des projets soutenus par l'IFC, 1996–2006

Le rôle de l'IFC en matière de développement ressort clairement de ses Statuts et de sa mission. L'Article 1 stipule que l'IFC « s'efforcera de stimuler et de promouvoir les conditions favorisant le courant du capital privé local et étranger vers des investissements de caractère productif dans les pays membres ». Dans le but de produire un impact sur le développement, l'IFC poursuit quatre objectifs principaux : promouvoir des marchés ouverts et compétitifs, appuyer les entreprises et autres partenaires du secteur privé, générer des emplois productifs et fournir des services de base, et créer des opportunités pour permettre aux populations d'échapper à la pauvreté et d'améliorer leurs conditions de vie. L'IFC poursuit son action de développement en ayant recours à deux instruments : les produits financiers et les services-conseil.

Depuis 1991, l'IFC a approximativement sextuplé ses activités de financement et a investi environ 50 milliards de dollars dans des pays en développement dans le cadre de ses opérations de prêt et ses prises de participations. Si l'on prend en compte les montants qu'elle a mobilisés sous forme de cofinancements, les projets appuyés par l'IFC ont systématiquement absorbé l'équivalent d'environ 4 % du total des entrées de capitaux privés dans les pays en développement. La proportion des investissements de l'IFC destinés aux pays qu'elle considère *pionniers* — c'est-à-dire des pays à faible revenu (tels que définis par la Banque) et/ou présentant des risques élevés[2] — est deux fois plus élevée que celle des investissements étrangers directs allant à ces pays. Les investissements de l'IFC représentent également environ 30 % des volumes alloués au secteur privé par les institutions financières internationales. Pendant cette période, la Banque mondiale a accordé aux gouvernements des pays en développement une aide à hauteur de 340 milliards de dollar environ, affichant des variations bien moins prononcées en glissement annuel que celle de l'IFC.

La majorité des projets évalués ont été jugés avoir un fort impact sur le développement

Sur les 627 opérations d'investissement approuvées durant la période 1991-2001 et évaluées entre 1996 et 2006 (une fois que les projets ont atteint leur régime de croisière)[3], 59 % des projets (65 % en volume) ont été jugés avoir un fort impact sur le développement. En d'autres termes, la plupart des projets affichent dans l'ensemble des résultats durables (qui devraient perdurer à long terme) pour l'ensemble des indicateurs de performance aux plans financier, économique, environnemental et social — tout en contribuant t au développement général du secteur privé. Ces résultats traduisent en partie le fait que les projets de l'IFC subissent l'épreuve du marché, de sorte qu'ils ne peuvent pas être directement comparés avec ceux d'institutions de développement dont les activités sont axées sur le secteur public comme la Banque mondiale[4]. Les performances varient considérablement selon les secteurs et les régions ; les résultats des projets appuyés par l'IFC sont moins bons en Afrique que dans d'autres régions en grande partie parce que le climat des affaires y est moins favorable et que les clients de l'IFC y respectent moins les normes environnementales et sociales.

Rentabilité et résultats au plan du développement vont habituellement de pair

Outre qu'il évalue l'impact sur le développement des projets soutenus par l'IFC, IEG examine si ses opérations d'investissement contribuent à assurer la rentabilité de l'IFC elle-même (et donc sa

capacité de financer ses opérations futures à partir des bénéfices mis en réserve). Pour qu'une note élevée soit attribuée au titre de la rentabilité de l'investissement, il faut pouvoir compter, s'il s'agit d'un prêt, qu'il sera remboursé conformément au calendrier établi et, s'il s'agit d'une prise de participation, qu'elle aura un taux de rendement supérieur à celui d'un prêt compte tenu du risque supplémentaire qu'elle comporte. Bien que la proportion des prises de participation affichant de bons résultats à cet égard (31 % ont produit des rendements supérieurs à la référence, contre 74 % des prêts), celles qui sont jugées profitables contribuent aux bons rendements du portefeuille global de l'IFC.

Lorsque l'on considère à la fois la rentabilité des opérations de l'IFC et leur impact sur le développement, la moitié environ des projets de l'IFC évalués pendant la période de 1996 à 2006 affichent une double note *élevé-élevée* (un impact élevé du projet au plan du développement et une rentabilité de l'investissement acceptable jugée par l'IFC) tandis qu'environ un tiers des projets affichent une double note *faible-faible* (ils ont un faible impact sur le développement et ont une rentabilité jugée moins qu'acceptable pour l'IFC). On peut en déduire que l'IFC n'a pas cherché à appuyer des projets pour lesquels il importait de trouver un compromis entre l'impact sur le développement et la rentabilité de l'investissement. La note *élevé-élevée* peut ne pas être attribuée à un projet pour diverses raisons, notamment le risque de marché associé à différentes branches d'activité, un climat des affaires défavorable, des entités parrainantes présentant des insuffisances ou la qualité insuffisante des travaux de l'IFC.

Il est difficile d'évaluer précisément l'efficacité de l'action de l'IFC au plan du développement

L'IFC a entrepris d'améliorer considérablement la façon dont elle mesure l'impact sur le développement au niveau des projets, mais il lui faudra encore résoudre des problèmes méthodologiques pour pouvoir pleinement identifier son efficacité globale en matière de développement au niveau sectoriel, de même qu'à l'échelle nationale, régionale et mondiale. Les systèmes de suivi et d'autoévaluation de l'IFC ont été perfectionnés de sorte que l'institution commence à mesurer ses résultats de développement pour l'ensemble de son portefeuille d'opérations d'investissement et de services-conseil (essentiellement grâce à un système de suivi de l'impact de ses opérations d'investissement mis en place en 2005). Sur cette base, les systèmes devront évoluer de manière à permettre de prendre en compte les impacts plus vastes des projets bénéficiant de l'appui de l'IFC au niveau sectoriel et à l'échelle nationale.

Les efforts d'harmonisation des normes d'évaluation du secteur privé utilisées par les institutions de développement multilatérales progressent. S'ils ont bien débouché sur l'adoption d'un ensemble de normes de bonne pratique, que suit de manière générale l'IFC, il reste difficile de comparer la performance de la Société à celles d'autres institutions internationales de financement du secteur privé, ne serait-ce que parce qu'elles ont une mission et des objectifs institutionnels différents.

Les leçons tirées de l'évaluation du développement du secteur privé sur une période de dix ans

Cinq facteurs contribuent à déterminer les résultats des projets

Il n'existe pas de formule magique qui garantisse que toutes les opérations de l'IFC produiront un développement durable du secteur privé. Il ressort néanmoins des évaluations réalisées sur une période de dix ans que cinq facteurs ont un impact considérable sur les résultats obtenus par l'IFC au plan du développement au niveau de ses projets :

- l'évolution de la qualité du climat des affaires dans un pays après l'approbation d'un projet ;
- le secteur d'activité dans lequel un investissement est réalisé ;
- la qualité de l'entité parrainante ;
- le niveau de développement du marché pour les produits, la société cliente et les risques liés au type de projet ; et
- la qualité des interventions de l'IFC.

La mesure dans laquelle l'IFC peut proposer des financements en monnaie nationale, directement ou indirectement, aux petites et moyennes en-

treprises, et la nature des liens entre les services-conseil et les activités d'investissement ont aussi des conséquences importantes pour le développement du secteur privé.

La qualité des interventions de l'IFC est un facteur d'une importance majeure

La qualité de l'exécution et de la supervision des projets par l'IFC (surtout en ce qui concerne leurs effets environnementaux et sociaux) est le facteur le plus déterminant des résultats des projets appuyés par l'IFC en matière de développement. C'est le cas tout particulièrement en Afrique, où l'IFC a parfois atténué les risques très élevés associés au climat des affaires grâce à des travaux préparatoires minutieux et une conception bien adaptée des projets. Toutefois, la qualité des interventions de l'IFC est généralement moins bien notée en Afrique que dans les autres régions (la qualité a été jugée élevée dans 45 % des opérations menées en Afrique, contre 68 % des opérations effectuées dans d'autres régions), ce qui montre que l'IFC est généralement disposée à prendre des risques plus importants dans la région et témoigne de la difficulté de recruter, de former et de conserver un personnel doté d'une expérience suffisante.

Les implications stratégiques pour l'IFC

L'IFC a, dans l'ensemble, effectué de bons choix stratégiques mais des problèmes persistent

Les conclusions des évaluations effectuées au cours des dix dernières années confortent les orientations et les priorités fondamentales de l'IFC. Les opérations entreprises dans des pays et des secteurs pionniers d'importance stratégique ont en général produit des résultats supérieurs à la moyenne et l'IFC a amélioré sa capacité de gestion des risques des projets au stade de l'approbation ainsi que la qualité globale de ses activités de supervision. Les conclusions de l'évaluation identifient cependant certaines sources potentielles de risques et d'opportunités pour l'IFC au regard des défis qu'elle s'est fixée dans ses *Notes d'orientation stratégique* 2006[5]. Au nombre de ces orientations, on peut citer un plus grand impact sur le développement, une coopération plus étroite avec les autres institutions du Groupe de la Banque mondiale, un rôle moteur dans la définition des normes, une amélioration de la satisfaction de ses clients, une assise financière solide et un personnel de haut calibre.

L'IFC doit cibler ses interventions plus précisément sur les pays, en particulier les pays à revenu intermédiaire

L'IFC a réussi à mobiliser des financements auprès d'une variété de bailleurs pour appuyer des opérations dans des pays présentant des risques élevés et à faible revenu afin de poursuivre sa stratégie axée sur les marchés pionniers. Elle pourrait désormais s'efforcer de mieux définir son rôle et ses priorités dans les pays à revenu intermédiaire non pionniers[6], où vit environ un tiers de ceux qui ont moins de deux dollars par jour pour subsister et où l'IFC réalise la plupart de ses opérations d'investissement. Compte tenu de la capacité insuffisante des des marchés des capitaux nationaux, de nombreux pays à revenu intermédiaire n'ont, dans le meilleur des cas, qu'un accès limité, comme les pays à faible revenu, à des capitaux à long terme en monnaie nationale ; de ce fait, les entreprises sont obligées de contracter des emprunts en devises, et sont donc de manière générale exposées au risque d'une dévaluation. Les infrastructures nécessaires aux activités de production et aux échanges sont un autre problème auquel se heurtent beaucoup de pays à revenu intermédiaire, tout comme l'élimination de vastes poches de pauvreté rurales. L'IFC a donc encore un rôle important à jouer dans de nombreux pays à revenu intermédiaire. Elle a toutefois obtenu des résultats médiocres au plan du développement lorsqu'elle a appuyé des projets dans ces pays sans que l'additionalité de sa contribution ait été clairement établie, ce qui montre que l'IFC doit bien comprendre la dynamique du développement du secteur privé d'un pays et identifier les domaines dans lesquels elle jouit d'un avantage comparatif de manière à pouvoir compléter efficacement les flux de capitaux existants.

Nécessité de mettre en place de nouvelles incitations et de nouveaux mécanismes de coopération pour le Groupe de la Banque mondiale

Un ciblage de ses interventions au niveau national permettrait à l'IFC de compléter les efforts qu'elle déploie aux niveaux sectoriel et régional, en partie en l'aidant à identifier les possibilités d'une coopération renforcée avec la Banque mondiale[7] dans des domaines où il existe des synergies comme l'amélioration du climat des affaires, le développement des circuits financiers, le développement des infrastructures et l'impact environnemental et social. Les travaux menés en collaboration dans ces domaines ont eu un impact positif sur le développement dans des pays aussi divers que le Mexique, les Philippines et le Sénégal, et ils revêtent une importance primordiale dans le cas de l'Afrique, qui a pris beaucoup de retard par rapport à d'autres marchés en développement. Dans la pratique, la coopération entre l'IFC et la Banque mondiale dans les domaines où il existe des synergies n'a pas été aussi étroite que prévu dans les Stratégies d'aide-pays (CAS), et les évaluations ont révélé autant de facteurs pouvant inhiber la coopération que de facteurs pouvant la favoriser. Les CAS ont rarement constitué un bon cadre de coopération ; il serait donc souhaitable de mettre en place de nouvelles mesures incitatives et de nouveaux mécanismes pour compléter ces dernières.

L'IFC doit veiller à la bonne qualité de ses interventions alors qu'elle poursuit son processus de décentralisation

La stratégie actuelle de l'IFC vise à accroître son impact en termes de développement en élargissant l'ampleur de ses opérations d'investissement et de services-conseil et en étant plus présente sur le terrain grâce à la poursuite de la décentralisation de ses activités. La Société devra être pleinement consciente des compromis qu'elle pourrait devoir accepter entre une rapide expansion, les transformations organisationnelles et la qualité de l'exécution des projets. Lorsqu'elle a procédé à un profond remaniement de sa structure en 1998–2001, la qualité des activités de supervision a chuté. L'IFC doit déjà veiller à conserver son personnel et à maintenir son savoir institutionnel de manière efficace, et les difficultés qu'elle peut rencontrer à ces égards iront en s'aggravant avec la poursuite du processus de décentralisation. Elle pourrait profiter des leçons de l'expérience de la Banque mondiale en matière de gestion du savoir dans le cadre de structures fortement décentralisées.

L'expérience montre la rapidité avec laquelle les marchés peuvent retirer leur soutien financier aux entreprises lorsque surviennent des problèmes économiques ou politiques défavorables. Malgré l'optimiste dont font preuve les investisseurs dans une grande partie du monde en développement, l'IFC pourrait clairement définir sa stratégie de manière à faire face à la menace d'une contraction des investissements à l'échelle mondiale, à l'impact probable de cette contraction sur ses clients et à considérer toute mesure d'atténuation qui pourrait s'avérer nécessaire. Planifier d'ores et déjà les dispositions à prendre pour améliorer les systèmes de gestion des risques et mettre au point de nouveaux produits d'atténuation des risques pour amortir les impacts sur ses clients renforcerait la capacité de l'IFC de faire face à de futurs chocs économiques et de conforter son rôle de stabilisation conjoncturelle.

Recommandations

Pour relever les nombreux défis auxquels la SFI se trouve confrontée, son équipe de direction devra mettre en œuvre les recommandations suivantes (décrites plus en détail au chapitre 4).

- Pour ses clients et parties prenantes,
  i) elle devra adopter des stratégies mieux adaptées au contexte national pour compléter son approche axée sur les secteurs et les régions, notamment en élaborant et en utilisant une série d'indicateurs du développement du secteur privé propre à chaque pays ;
  ii) dans le cadre de ses stratégies par pays, elle devra signaler les opportunités de traiter les questions indissociables de la pauvreté rurale et de la gestion durable des ressources naturelles dont les populations pauvres sont tributaires ; et identifier et développer des projets d'agroindustrie et de microfinance rurale ayant un fort impact et pouvant avoir de vastes effets de dé-

monstration, tout en menant les efforts de promotion de pratiques durables dans les domaines social et environnemental.
- Au niveau des procédures internes, elle devra coopérer davantage avec la Banque mondiale dans les domaines où il est possible d'exploiter des synergies,
  i) en examinant, avec la Banque, de nouvelles incitations et de nouveaux mécanismes de coopération pour compléter le processus des CAS ;
  ii) en identifiant au stade de l'approbation les investissements qui ont été facilités par l'assistance fournie par la Banque dans le domaine de l'action publique ou du cadre réglementaire et en assurant leur suivi durant tout le cycle du projet (grâce au système de suivi des réalisations au plan du développement ou par d'autres moyens) pour déterminer leurs résultats.
- Du point de vue du capital humain, l'IFC devra suivre attentivement le déroulement du processus de décentralisation pour s'assurer que la qualité de ses interventions demeure satisfaisante et que les nouveaux chargés d'investissement bénéficient d'un programme de formation rigoureux.
- S'agissant du financement et de l'évaluation,
  i) l'IFC devra systématiquement s'efforcer d'améliorer ses systèmes de gestion du risque et se préparer à faire face à la prochaine correction sur les marchés internationaux, notamment peut-être en utilisant de manière plus générale des produits d'atténuation des risques et en formulant de nouveaux.
  ii) l'IFC devra, avec l'appui d'IEG, développer son système d'indicateurs pour mieux déterminer les impacts plus généraux des projets soutenus par l'IFC au plan sectoriel et à l'échelle nationale, et en tirer les enseignements nécessaires.

Resumen

Ésta es la décima revisión anual de la Corporación Financiera Internacional (IFC, por su sigla en inglés) que realiza el Grupo de Evaluación Independiente (GEI)[1]. En cada revisión, el GEI evalúa el desempeño de la IFC en la promoción del desarrollo sustentable del sector privado en los países en desarrollo. La revisión de 2007 le ofrece al GEI la oportunidad de analizar retrospectivamente una década de resultados para las operaciones de la IFC en el sector privado y preguntarse

- Si los proyectos respaldados por la IFC lograron resultados sólidos en términos de desarrollo financiero, económico, ambiental y social;
- Qué se aprendió acerca del desarrollo del sector privado luego de 10 años de evaluación, y
- Si hay consecuencias estratégicas para la IFC en la mejora de su desempeño en términos de desarrollo en los próximos años.

Resultados en términos de desarrollo de los proyectos respaldados por la IFC, 1996–2006

El rol de la IFC en relación con el desarrollo está claramente establecido en su Convenio Constitutivo y en su Misión. El Artículo 1 establece que la IFC "tratará de estimular y de ayudar a la creación de condiciones que favorezcan el flujo de capital privado, local y extranjero, hacia una inversión productiva en los países miembros". Para generar un impacto en términos de desarrollo, la IFC lleva a cabo una misión con cuatro facetas: la promoción de mercados abiertos y competitivos, el

apoyo a empresas y a otros asociados del sector privado, la generación de puestos de trabajo productivos y la prestación de servicios básicos, y la creación de oportunidades para que las personas escapen de la pobreza y mejoren sus vidas. La IFC utiliza dos tipos de intervención para el desarrollo: los instrumentos financieros y la asistencia de asesoría.

Desde 1991, la IFC ha aumentado sus actividades financieras aproximadamente seis veces, con una inversión de cerca de US$50.000 millones en países en desarrollo, a través de sus operaciones de préstamos e inversiones en capital social. Si se incluyen los fondos provistos por cofinanciadores, los proyectos respaldados por la IFC han representado de manera sostenida cerca del 4% de todos los flujos de capital privado hacia países en desarrollo. Las inversiones de la IFC tienen más del doble de concentración que la inversión extranjera directa en los países que la institución denomina "de frontera" (aquéllos que el Banco

Mundial define como "país de ingreso bajo" y/o países de alto riesgo)[2]. Las inversiones de la IFC también representan cerca del 30% de los volúmenes del sector privado en la Institución Financiera Internacional. El Banco Mundial suministró aproximadamente US$340.000 millones en concepto de asistencia para los gobiernos de países en desarrollo durante este período, con cambios año a año en los volúmenes mucho más estáticos que los de la IFC.

La mayoría de los proyectos evaluados logró altas calificaciones de desarrollo

De las 627 operaciones de inversión aprobadas durante el período 1991–2001 y evaluadas entre 1996 y 2006 (a medida que los proyectos alcanzaban la madurez operativa)[3], el 59% (un 65% en términos de volumen) logró altas calificaciones de desarrollo a nivel de los proyectos. En otras palabras, la mayoría de los proyectos, en términos generales, generó resultados sostenibles (y se espera que sigan generándolos a largo plazo) en relación con los indicadores que miden el desempeño financiero, económico, ambiental y social, además de contribuir en general con el desarrollo del sector privado. Estos resultados reflejan en parte la prueba de mercado que enfrentan los proyectos de la IFC, es decir, que no pueden compararse directamente con los de instituciones de desarrollo orientadas al sector público, como el Banco Mundial[4]. El desempeño ha variado en forma significativa entre los distintos sectores y regiones: por ejemplo, los proyectos respaldados por la IFC en África estuvieron rezagados respecto de los de otras regiones, principalmente debido a ambientes más desafiantes para los negocios y al menor cumplimiento ambiental y social entre los clientes de la IFC.

El impacto en términos de desarrollo y la rentabilidad suele producirse en forma conjunta

Además de evaluar los resultados en términos de desarrollo de los proyectos respaldados por la IFC, el GEI también analiza si las operaciones de inversión contribuyen en forma positiva con la propia rentabilidad de la IFC (y, por lo tanto, con su capacidad para financiar proyectos futuros a partir de utilidades no distribuidas). A fin de lograr

un mayor nivel de retorno sobre la inversión, debe esperarse que un préstamo se reembolse en el tiempo estipulado, mientras que una inversión en capital debería suministrar a la IFC un retorno superior al de un préstamo, proporcional al riesgo extra que implica el vehículo. Aunque son menos las inversiones en capital que se consideran exitosas en estos términos (un 31% registró retornos por encima de los puntos de referencia, proporción que en el caso de los préstamos fue de un 74%), aquéllas que en efecto se consideran exitosas contribuyeron con los elevados retornos generales de la cartera de la IFC.

Cuando se analizan los resultados de inversión de las operaciones de la IFC junto con los resultados de los proyectos en términos de desarrollo, cerca de la mitad de estos proyectos evaluados durante el período 1996–2006 recibió calificaciones *alta-alta* (calificaciones altas en términos de desarrollo a nivel de los proyectos y un retorno sobre la inversión de la IFC aceptable), mientras que un tercio recibió calificaciones *baja-baja* (resultados pobres en términos de desarrollo y retorno sobre la inversión de la IFC por debajo de lo aceptable). Esto muestra que la IFC no ha respaldado activamente los proyectos donde había un desequilibrio entre los resultados en términos de desarrollo y los retornos sobre la inversión. Son varias las causas por las que los proyectos no logran calificaciones *alta-alta*: los riesgos comerciales inherentes de distintos sectores industriales, ambientes adversos para los negocios, baja calidad de los patrocinadores o deficiencia en la calidad del trabajo de la IFC.

La evaluación integral de la eficacia en términos de desarrollo de la IFC constituye un desafío

Si bien la IFC está logrando mejoras significativas en relación con la forma de medir el desempeño en términos de desarrollo a nivel de los proyectos, aún debe resolver algunos desafíos metodológicos antes de determinar su eficacia en términos de desarrollo general a niveles sectoriales, nacionales, regionales e internacionales. Los sistemas de control y autoevaluación de la IFC han progresado a punto tal que la IFC está comenzando a medir sus resultados de desarrollo en toda su cartera de operaciones de asesoría e inversión (principalmente a través de un sistema de seguimiento de sus operaciones introducido en 2005). Sobre la base de ese progreso, estos sistemas tendrán que evolucionar para reflejar los efectos más amplios (a nivel sectorial y regional) de los proyectos que apoya la IFC.

Se ha registrado un progreso gradual al momento de armonizar los estándares con los que las instituciones multilaterales de desarrollo evalúan el sector privado. Si bien esto ha generado un conjunto consensuado de estándares de prácticas modelo respecto del cual la IFC muestra un elevado grado de cumplimiento, la comparación del desempeño de la IFC con la de otras instituciones financieras internacionales del sector privado sigue siendo un desafío, debido en gran parte a las diferencias que existen entre los cometidos y los objetivos de las instituciones.

Lecciones extraídas de los 10 años de evaluación del desarrollo del sector privado

Los cinco factores que han intervenido en el desempeño de los proyectos

No existe una fórmula mágica que garantice un desarrollo sostenible del sector privado en todas las operaciones de la IFC. Sin embargo, tras 10 años de evaluación, todo indica que hay cinco factores que influyen significativamente sobre el desempeño de la IFC en términos de desarrollo a nivel de los proyectos:

- Cambios en la calidad del ambiente para los negocios de un país luego de la aprobación del proyecto;
- Tipo de sector industrial en el que se hace una inversión;
- Calidad del patrocinador;
- Nivel de riesgos del mercado del producto, de la empresa cliente y del tipo de proyecto, y
- Calidad del trabajo de la IFC.

Existen otros factores que tienen importantes consecuencias para el desarrollo del sector privado: hasta qué punto la IFC puede ofrecer opciones en moneda nacional, si ofrece financiamiento en forma directa o indirecta a pequeñas y medianas empresas y el carácter de la integración entre los servicios de asesoría y las actividades de inversión.

La calidad del trabajo de la IFC ha sido muy importante

La calidad de la ejecución y la supervisión de proyectos por parte de la IFC (en especial de los efectos sociales y ambientales) ha representado la influencia más crítica sobre los resultados en términos de desarrollo de los proyectos respaldados por la IFC. Esto es especialmente claro en África, donde la IFC, en algunos casos, ha logrado mitigar riesgos muy altos en el ambiente para los negocios mediante un procedimiento de diligencia debida de calidad y una estructuración de proyectos adecuada. Sin embargo, la calidad del trabajo de la IFC, en general, se ha visto retrasada respecto de otras regiones (la calidad del trabajo se calificó como "alta" en el 45% de las operaciones de África, proporción que llegó al 68% en las operaciones realizadas en otras regiones), lo cual resalta los mayores riesgos que la IFC ha estado dispuesta a aceptar históricamente en la región, además de reflejar los desafíos al momento de contratar, capacitar y retener personal con experiencia adecuada.

Consecuencias estratégicas para la IFC

En general, la IFC ha tomado decisiones estratégicas acertadas, pero aún quedan desafíos

Los resultados de la evaluación de la última década apoyan, en general, las orientaciones estratégicas y las prioridades de la IFC. Las operaciones en países y sectores de frontera estratégicos presentaron, en su mayoría, resultados superiores al promedio en términos de desarrollo, mientras que la IFC logró un mejor equilibrio entre los riesgos del proyecto al momento de la aprobación y una mejor supervisión general de los proyectos. Al mismo tiempo, los resultados de la evaluación también resaltan algunas posibles áreas de riesgos y oportunidades para la IFC en el contexto de los desafíos que se planteó en su documento de *Orientación Estratégica* de 2006[5], tales como mayor impacto en términos de desarrollo, mejor cooperación con el Grupo del Banco Mundial, liderazgo al momento de definir estándares, mejor satisfacción del cliente, finanzas sólidas y personal capacitado.

La IFC debe desarrollar un enfoque más específico para cada país, en especial en países de ingreso mediano

La IFC ha logrado movilizar financiamiento de una variedad de fuentes para apoyar operaciones en países de alto riesgo e ingreso dentro del marco de su estrategia con respecto a los países de frontera. La IFC podría tratar ahora de definir con mayor exactitud su rol y sus prioridades en países de ingreso mediano no calificados como "de frontera"[6], donde vive aproximadamente un tercio de las personas que subsisten con menos de dos dólares por día y donde la IFC realiza la mayor parte de sus operaciones de inversión. La falta de capacidad en los mercados financieros internos implica que muchos países de ingreso mediano se asemejan a países de ingreso bajo porque tienen una disponibilidad nula o reducida de financiamiento en moneda nacional a largo plazo, a raíz de lo cual la exposición al riesgo de devaluación pasa a ser un problema generalizado para las empresas que se ven obligadas a pedir préstamos en moneda extranjera. La infraestructura que respalda la producción y el comercio constituye otro desafío en muchos países de ingreso mediano, como lo es enfrentar el problema de los grandes focos de pobreza rural. Por lo tanto, aún existe una función valiosa que puede cumplir la IFC en muchos países de ingreso mediano. Sin embargo, la IFC ha conseguido resultados muy débiles en términos de desarrollo cuando brindó apoyo a proyectos en los que la adicionalidad en países de ingreso mediano no estaba clara, lo cual enfatiza la necesidad de que la IFC comprenda claramente la dinámica de desarrollo en el sector privado en un país y determine dónde están sus ventajas comparativas, a fin de poder complementar con eficacia los flujos de capital existentes.

Se necesitan nuevos incentivos y mecanismos para la cooperación dentro del Grupo del Banco Mundial

Un enfoque más específico para cada país podría complementar las iniciativas sectoriales y regionales de la IFC, lo cual permitiría en parte detectar oportunidades de mejorar la cooperación con el Banco Mundial[7] en áreas de sinergia como la mejora del ambiente para los negocios, la profundización de la capacidad del sector financiero, el desarrollo de infraestructura y el impacto ambiental y social. La cooperación en estas áreas ha traído mejoras en el desarrollo en países tan diversos como Filipinas, México y Senegal, y es extremadamente importante en África, región que se ha rezagado respecto de otros mercados en desarrollo. En la práctica, la cooperación entre la IFC y el Banco Mundial en áreas de sinergia no ha alcanzado el nivel previsto en las Estrategias de Asistencia a los Países (EAP), y las evaluaciones determinaron que existen tantos factores que obstaculizan la cooperación como factores que la promueven. En general, las EAP no han suministrado un buen marco para la cooperación, por lo que sería bueno contar con nuevos incentivos y mecanismos para complementarlas.

La IFC debe asegurar una sólida calidad de trabajo a la par de la descentralización

La estrategia actual de la IFC busca un mayor impacto en términos de desarrollo a través de la intensificación de las operaciones del servicio de asesoría y la inversión, y una representación local más sólida por medio de una mayor descentralización de las operaciones de la IFC. La IFC deberá estar consciente de los posibles equilibrios entre el rápido crecimiento, la reestructuración y la calidad de la ejecución de los proyectos. Durante un período anterior de considerables cambios institucionales en 1998-2001, la calidad de la supervisión disminuyó drásticamente. La retención efectiva del personal y los conocimientos ya son áreas que requieren atención, y estos desafíos se magnifican con la mayor descentralización. La IFC podría aprender de las experiencias del Banco Mundial en la gestión de los conocimientos bajo estructuras altamente descentralizadas.

La experiencia pone de relieve cómo los mercados pueden retirar rápidamente el apoyo financiero para las empresas en respuesta a los acontecimientos políticos o económicos adversos. Pese al actual optimismo respecto de la inversión entre los inversores de gran parte del mundo en desarrollo, la IFC podría tratar explícitamente en su estrategia la amenaza de un descenso global de la inversión, sus posibles efectos para los clientes y cualquier medida que pueda ser necesaria para mitigarlos. Planificar ahora la mejora de los sistemas de gestión del riesgo y desarrollar nuevos productos para mitigar los riesgos y así amortiguar los efectos para los clientes fortalecería la capacidad de la IFC de responder a los futuros impactos económicos, y también incrementaría su rol contracíclico.

Recomendaciones

Para abordar los diversos desafíos que enfrenta la institución, la administración de la IFC deberá seguir las siguientes recomendaciones (véase el capítulo 4 para obtener información más detallada).

- Desde una perspectiva de clientes y partes interesadas,
  i) Adoptar estrategias de país más personalizadas, para complementar su sólido enfoque sectorial y regional, incluso a través del desarrollo y la búsqueda de una serie de indicadores de desarrollo del sector privado específicos para cada país.
  ii) En sus estrategias de país, resaltar las oportunidades para trabajar en el vínculo entre la pobreza rural y los recursos naturales sostenibles, del que depende la población pobre, y para identificar y desarrollar negocios agrícolas de alto impacto y proyectos de microfinanzas rurales con efectos de demostración generalizada, y al mismo tiempo proporcionar el liderazgo para fo-

mentar prácticas ambiental y socialmente sostenibles.
- Desde una perspectiva de proceso interno, incrementar la cooperación con el Banco Mundial en las áreas de sinergia
  i) Analizando, junto con el Banco, nuevos incentivos y mecanismos de cooperación para complementar el proceso de EAP.
  ii) Identificando inversiones en proceso de aprobación que fueron facilitadas por el asesoramiento del Banco a un gobierno en materia de regulación o políticas, y supervisándolas a lo largo del ciclo del proyecto (a través del Sistema de Seguimiento de Operaciones de la IFC o por otros medios) para evaluar su éxito.
- Desde una perspectiva de capital humano, controlar de cerca el proceso de descentralización para asegurar que la calidad del trabajo de la IFC se mantenga sólida y se vea respaldada por un riguroso programa de capacitación para el nuevo personal de inversión.
- Desde una perspectiva de la medición y las finanzas,
  i) Realizar esfuerzos duraderos para mejorar sus sistemas de gestión del riesgo y prepararse para la próxima corrección en los mercados internacionales, incluyendo quizás el uso extendido y el desarrollo de nuevos productos para mitigar los riesgos.
  ii) Con el respaldo del GEI, mejorar sus indicadores para comprender mejor los impactos en el sector más amplio y en los países de los proyectos que respalda la IFC, y aprender de ellos.

IFC Management Response to IEG-IFC

Independent Evaluation of IFC's
Development Results 2007: Lessons and
Implications from 10 Years of Experience*

Management greatly welcomes IEG-IFC's tenth, independent, annual review of evaluation findings. This year's annual review takes stock of eleven years of project approvals, from 1991 to 2001 (evaluated in 1996–2006).

Introduction

Management notes that IEG-IFC's independent evaluation found that IFC had positive development impacts and profitable investment operations. The report indicates that most of IFC's projects have consistently performed well in terms of financial, economic, environmental, and social aspects, and have had good impacts on private sector development. This performance was achieved while IFC's projects were exposed to all the risks that are associated with private sector investments in the developing world.

We are encouraged by IEG-IFC's independent finding that IFC has generally made sound corporate-wide strategic choices. The report found that IFC has successfully scaled up its investment and ad-

visory operations in frontier counties (high risk and low income) and in priority sectors, such as infrastructure. More importantly, the report shows that investment operations have largely yielded above-average development results in these priority areas.

We also note that the report indicates that impacts on private sector development of IFC's projects have been strong and reached well beyond the project company. Among other results, these projects had broad positive demonstration effects, stimulating follow-on investments by other investors, downstream and upstream business linkages, and increased competition. Some contributed to domestic capital markets development by providing increased access to finance and introducing new financing instruments.

The report also found a consistently strong positive correlation between development and investment results. This supports IFC's long-standing

---

* Distributed to IFC's Board of Directors on April 11, 2007, and discussed by the Board's Committee on Development Effectiveness on April 25, 2007. Released by IFC in accordance with IFC's Policy on Disclosure of Information.

operating principle of pursuing projects that are both developmentally and financially viable over the long term.

IFC takes on more risks than other investors, catalyzing private investments where the private sector would not go alone. In some markets, such as in Sub-Saharan Africa, IFC took on higher country risks, in line with its development agenda. The evaluation findings should be interpreted in this context, recognizing that success rates will reflect the higher risks the Corporation undertakes.

The 1991–2006 period in which the evaluated projects operated saw major financial crises, including those in Asia, Argentina, Mexico, Russia, Turkey, and Brazil. IFC remained focused during these years of high risk and market volatility, quickly responding to crises through countercyclical investments, as well as enhanced portfolio operations to support its existing clients. This allowed IFC to mobilize scarce capital for the private sector in difficult times and help boost liquidity in affected economies. At the same time, IFC remained forward-looking by pursuing a strategy to reach markets and sectors where it can deliver greater development impacts and strong additionality.

Looking forward, Management welcomes IEG-IFC's finding that more recent commitments are poised to have greater development impacts. The report indicates that IFC's overall work quality, a key driver of success, is on the uptrend and project risks are better mitigated. In addition, the improving investment climates in many countries where IFC operates suggests greater development results, given IEG-IFC's finding that development impacts are better when investment climates are improving. Nevertheless, as IFC continues to take on significant project risks, actual results will depend on many factors, including market performance.

Management recognizes that there may be opportunities for IFC to enhance its development effectiveness and finds this report valuable in informing IFC in this regard. Management agrees with the general direction of the report's recommendations. Specific responses to each recommendation follow.

Responses to Specific Recommendations

IEG-IFC Recommendation: Develop a deeper, more differentiated country approach.

As IFC decentralizes, it has the opportunity to adopt more tailored country strategies, to complement its strong sector and regional approach. This strategy might include, in consultation with the Bank and country governments, the development and pursuit of a set of country specific private sector development indicators (such as for the level of private, gross fixed capital formation; banking sector capacity; and private provision of infrastructure).

Management Response

Management agrees with the recommendation to develop a more differentiated country approach. Current IFC strategic processes already involve developing country level strategies that feed into Country Assistance Strategies (CASs) and into IFC's regional strategies that form part of IFC's Strategic Directions Paper. Because of the commonality of certain characteristics, regional departments are also able to group countries with similar needs and issues for the purpose of developing a coordinated approach. For example, in Sub-Saharan Africa, countries are grouped in four categories: (i) post-conflict (such as the Democratic Republic of Congo and Liberia); (ii) natural resource rich (such as Nigeria and Tanzania); (iii) middle income (such as South Africa and Mauritius); and (iv) others (such as Mali and Niger). Similar approaches are used in other regions.

Building on this base of activity, IFC is seeking to strengthen its country focus. As discussed in *IFC Strategic Directions, FY08-10: Creating Opportunity* (chapter 2), IFC is working to develop greater systemic approaches to its activities, which will be done at the country or sector level. In addition, increased IFC staff country presence through its phased decentralization should also facilitate a more country-focused strategic approach.

With respect to the suggestion to develop macro private sector development targets, we need to study this more carefully to determine what is feasible and meaningful, considering the difficulty in attributing country-wide macro indicators to IFC operations. IFC could also benefit from IEG-IFC findings on which private sector development target indicators have worked in other institutions.

In the meantime, IFC is working on advancing its metrics on outcomes and impacts that can clearly be attributed to IFC's projects, advisory activities, and systemic approaches. These metrics could serve as IFC targets, but they will have to be tried on perhaps one or two countries on a pilot basis. There may be some issues with respect to the burden on clients for certain types of reporting. Therefore, IFC will need to assess the feasibility of this approach.

In addition, IFC has on-going work with the World Bank in providing broad indicators that countries may use to track private sector development. The joint World Bank/IFC annual *Doing Business* report is one example which has been increasingly used by many countries in setting targets in their reform agenda for improving investment climates.

Another joint World Bank/IFC initiative in indicator-setting is the on-going development of the "Private Sector at a Glance" tables. These one-page per country tables cover almost 60 key private sector indicators encompassing: (i) economic and social context (such as inflation rate and size of labor force); (ii) investment climate (such as ease of doing business ranking and number of procedures to start a business); (iii) private sector investment (such as private participation in infrastructure and net private FDI); (iv) regulation and taxes (such as time dealing with government officials and corporate tax rate); (v) finance and banking (such as total financial system deposit and bank branches per one hundred thousand people); and (vi) infrastructure (such as paved roads and electric power outages).

IEG-IFC Recommendation: Place an emphasis on rural development.

In its country strategies, IFC may consider flagging opportunities to work on the nexus of rural poverty and sustainable natural resources, on which poor people depend, and to identify and develop high-impact agribusiness and rural microfinance projects with widespread demonstra-

tion effects, while simultaneously providing leadership in promoting socially and environmentally sustainable practices.

Management Response

In the FY08–10 Strategic Directions paper, IFC incorporated agribusiness into the five strategic priorities. Over the past five years, IFC's commitments in the agribusiness sector have grown significantly and development outcomes have also improved. IFC is now intending to further increase its involvement in this sector by, for example, developing wholesale financing solutions using financial intermediaries, processors, and traders.

IFC is also doing some rural microfinance. However, beyond agribusiness and a few rural microfinance projects, further study is needed to understand how to be effective in rural areas, given that the results so far appear to be mixed. Management would welcome IEG-IFC's input on lessons learned from successful models of private sector rural finance to inform this recommendation.

With respect to the suggestion of providing leadership to promote socially and environmentally sustainable practices, IFC addresses this through its sustainability pillar. Following Board approval and formal launch of the performance standards in 2006, IFC's focus has been on sound implementation of the performance standards. To maintain its environmental and social sustainability leadership, IFC will continue to provide support for the further adoption and implementation of the Equator Principles. In addition, IFC is committed to scaling up its activities in renewable energy and energy efficiency sectors.

IEG-IFC Recommendation: Pursue new incentives and mechanisms to enhance cooperation with the World Bank in areas of synergy.

To enhance cooperation with the World Bank in areas of synergy, IFC could (i) consider new incentives and mechanisms to complement the CAS process (with the Bank); and (ii) identify investments at approval that were facilitated by Bank policy or regulatory assistance and track them throughout the project cycle (through the

Development Outcome Tracking System (DOTS) or other means) in order to judge their success.

Management Response

Management agrees with the recommendation of enhancing cooperation with the Bank. Leveraging the strengths of the whole World Bank Group will become more important as IFC aims to increase its development impact and increase its systemic interventions. In past years, IFC has taken several steps in this direction, from increased focus by IFC Senior Management (including inviting senior World Bank staff to IFC's strategy discussions), to including World Bank Group cooperation as part of the performance appraisal for managers in Sub-Saharan Africa, to a World Bank Group review of advisory services to assess synergies. In addition, the World Bank and IFC have a joint Vice Presidency Unit (VPU) for Financial and Private Sector Development; the Vice President of this VPU is also IFC's Chief Economist. There are also joint departments in a number of core sectors: oil, gas, mining, information and communication technology, and subnationals.

Going forward, IFC envisages increasing cooperation with the World Bank as the Corporation adopts systemic and programmatic approaches to scaling up activities. Typically, a systemic approach to a sector would start with upstream advisory work on the business-enabling environment and/or privatization, often building on efforts of the World Bank and the government. IFC can then participate in the financing of associated projects, as appropriate. In addition, IFC and World Bank cooperation will be enhanced by the implementation of IFC's phased decentralization program. This should provide more opportunities for increased World Bank-IFC staff contacts in the field.

With respect to the recommendation to identify and track performance of investments with World Bank/IFC cooperation, IFC will consider this along with the other work it is doing on metrics, such as DOTS, systemic metrics, and advisory metrics. An important issue to consider is the extent to which the performance of projects can be partly attributed to good World Bank Group cooperation.

IEG-IFC Recommendation: Manage the trade-offs inherent in the decentralization process to achieve the highest possible work quality.

IFC will need to monitor the decentralization process closely to ensure that its work quality remains robust, and support this with a rigorous training program for new investment staff.

Management Response

Management agrees with the recommendation of ensuring that work quality remains high as IFC implements its phased decentralization. IFC is taking a number of steps to help ensure sustained work quality. More experienced/senior industry staff will be located in regional operations centers to mentor and provide leadership to more junior investment staff. Credit officer(s) will similarly be stationed in operations centers and will be involved in field-based investment decisions. Field presence of environment and social specialists will be increased to further mainstream sustainability into IFC's investment work, mitigate environmental and social risks, and ensure sustainability in clients' operations. In addition, as discussed below, IFC is undertaking several steps to enhance its risk management function in connection with the decentralization. Finally, the decentralization is being undertaken in a phased approach, first in Asia, and then in other regions over three years. This approach allows IFC to learn from experience and revise implementation processes, as needed, based on these experiences.

IFC is also developing a knowledge management initiative to maintain global expertise as decentralization deepens. This would include department-level training at entry (on-boarding) and structured activities for sharing knowledge. This initiative would complement the current IFC induction program and credit courses, which have proven to be effective.

IEG-IFC Recommendation: Ensure sound risk-management systems and develop risk-mitigation products.

IFC will need to make continued efforts to improve its risk-management systems and to prepare for the next correction in the international markets, including perhaps the extended use and development of new risk-mitigation products.

Management Response

Management agrees with this recommendation. IFC has in the past responded well to such crises by supporting its portfolio projects and undertaking countercyclical investments such as trade financing, as well as debt and equity funding. IFC's FY08-10 Strategic Directions paper acknowledges that current conditions in markets where it operates could change should there be financial crises. IFC's growth strategy takes into consideration the need to maintain financial capacity to accommodate the impact of possible financial crises. IFC stands ready to play a countercyclical role, with instruments such as trade lines and other support, including advisory services, to select clients.

IFC is undertaking several steps to improve overall risk management and thereby better prepare IFC for the next crises. As part of the decentralization initiative, the risk-management function will be transformed to facilitate improved client service and efficiency, while retaining appropriate checks and balances on decentralized decision making. Steps in this direction include: (i) the ongoing Business Process Review to streamline and strengthen operational procedures; (ii) shifting credit review and, eventually, most aspects of risk management decision-making to the field; (iii) enhanced corporate tools for risk management, including improved risk-rating systems; (iv) integration of development-impact metrics with financial risk-return metrics; (v) enhanced reporting of all metrics; and (vi) strengthening of information technology (IT) for more efficient and effective document processing and management.

IEG-IFC Recommendation: Strengthen the capacity for evaluation and its application.

As it deepens its self-evaluation and monitoring systems, IFC could, with IEG-IFC's assistance, advance its metrics to better understand (and derive lessons about) the wider sector and the country-level impacts of its operations.

Management Response

IFC agrees with the recommendation of deepening its evaluation and monitoring system in consultation with IEG-IFC. In the past, IFC has consulted with IEG-IFC on the development of its monitoring and self-evaluation system, that is, DOTS for investment operations and the project completion report (PCR) for advisory services. Both DOTS and PCRs are already contributing to increased development focus through clear objective-setting and tracking of outcomes. The PCR for advisory services, which is in the pilot stage, is being supplemented by thematic impact evaluations.

As the report mentions, DOTS is starting to supplement expanded project supervision reports (XPSRs) by providing results that cover IFC's entire portfolio (rather than a sample) and are more up-to-date. DOTS provides an earlier, preliminary indication of results, and takes into account developments after the XPSR is written. The data from DOTS feed into IFC's strategic decision making. Both XPSRs and DOTS already cover broader impacts beyond the client company.

On evaluating country and sector-wide impacts of IFC's operations and drawing lessons from them, IFC already routinely considers the results of its projects, including impacts beyond the client company. IEG-IFC's country and sector evaluations are also providing valuable insights. Tracking country and sector-wide metrics will, however, not make sense in all cases, because IFC's investments are often a relatively small share of private investment, making attribution of country-level results to IFC's activities difficult or even meaningless. However, as noted earlier, there could be scope for a pilot test.

Chairperson's Summary: Committee on Development Effectiveness (CODE)

On April 25, 2007 the Committee on Development Effectiveness (CODE) met to discuss the Independent Evaluation Group–IFC (IEG) report entitled *Independent Evaluation of IFC's Development Results 2007: Lessons and Implications from 10 Years of Experience* and the *Draft Management Response*.

Summary of Evaluation Report

This tenth IEG annual review of evaluation findings took stock of the performance of 627 investment operations approved during 1991–2001 and evaluated in 1996–2006, and drew on other evaluative materials to highlight lessons and strategic implications for IFC going forward. The report's main findings were: (i) 59 percent of IFC-supported projects (65 percent by volume) achieved high development ratings at the project level; (ii) development outcomes and IFC profitability tend to go hand in hand; (iii) five factors—changes in business climate; type of industry sector; quality of the sponsor; level of product market, client company, and project type risks; and IFC work quality—have significantly influenced the development outcomes of IFC-supported projects; and (iv) IFC has generally made sound strategic choices.

IEG recommended that IFC should: (1) develop a deeper, more differentiated country approach;

(2) place emphasis on rural development, especially through support for agribusiness and rural microfinance projects; (3) pursue new incentives and mechanisms to enhance cooperation with the Bank in areas of synergy; (4) manage the frictions resulting from a combination of the decentralization process, scaling up of operations, and improving work quality; (5) ensure sound risk management systems, and develop risk mitigation products for clients, to cope with the risks emanating from the next correction in the global financial market; and (6) strengthen the capacity for evaluation and its application.

Draft IFC Management Response

Management appreciated IEG's evaluation, and agreed with the general direction of its report's recommendations. It took note of the overall IEG finding that IFC has had positive development impact in most of its projects and profitable investment operations overall, and has made sound strategic decisions over the years. Management also noted the report's findings that quality at entry of recent commitments is likely to have better outcome than the evaluated sample, and the positive correlation between development impact and profitability. Management agreed on the importance of coordination with the Bank. It informed the meeting of its plans to hold an internal workshop to further consider the IEG's findings and recommendations, including the improvement of IFC measurement and evaluation system.

Overall Conclusions

Members commended IEG for the useful and informative report, and noted Management's general concurrence with the recommendations. They were reassured by Management that IFC's strategic directions incorporated the lessons distilled by IEG. One main issue discussed was measuring development impact and the related perceived trade-offs with profitability. While acknowledging the ongoing efforts in this area, speakers also commented on the need to improve the existing methodology to capture broader impacts, beyond financial and economic results. CODE noted that ex-post IFC profitability and development impact have tended to go together but also remarked on the IEG statement in the report that implies IFC support was limited for projects where there was a trade-off between the two.

CODE also considered risk mitigation instruments, and relative performance of equity vs. loan investments. Other issues discussed included the variability across sectors and regions, small vs. large projects, and aggregation of indicators to country or sector portfolios. Specific comments and questions were raised about IFC's role in middle-income countries (MICs), environmental and social practices, performance of intermediary operations, and evaluation criteria including those used for assessing additionality. Several speakers remarked on the expanded decentralization efforts, its implications on work quality including during the transition, and the challenges to management and Board oversight. It was hoped that decentralization would contribute to country focus. There were also comments on the different role of Country Assistance Strategies (CASs) in the Bank and IFC, the possibility of strengthening joint CASs, and the importance of paying due attention to private sector development in the overall Bank Group strategy.

Next Steps

Since the main topics of the IEG evaluation were central to the discussion of IFC strategic directions, CODE recommended that it be considered by the Board under an absence-of- objection procedure (without a meeting). For the future, members requested that the schedules be set to allow CODE to discuss the IEG report well before the discussion of IFC's strategic directions.

The following main issues were raised during the meetings:

Development impact. Speakers were generally satisfied with the overall positive link between developmental impact and profitability. However, they also took note of low development impact and low investment return in almost one-third of projects, and asked whether performance was linked to work quality, particularly at approval and supervision levels. Questions were also raised on how to address trade-offs between development and investment return. A few speakers sought more information on outsourcing supervision in projects with financial intermediaries. *Management pointed out that work quality has been improving in recent years based on IEG's report. Management also explained that the case of less than satisfactory work quality in the past was due to a number of reasons, including exogenous factors and certain opportunities or risks not being captured at the outset. Management also remarked that the critical stage for identifying development impact is project appraisal. Management indicated that IFC considers not only development impact, additionality, and financial viability, but also other factors such as quality of sponsors, or reputational risks.*

A number of members were concerned that the current methodology for measuring development impact was heavily focused on financial and economic results; there was a need to deepen assessment of qualitative impact; and development impacts at the sector, country, regional, and global levels were not being fully captured. Some speakers remarked on the perceived trade-offs between additionality and development impact, although there was a sentiment in favor of a more in-depth discussion of this issue at the subsequent meeting on IFC's strategic directions. *IEG indicated that the evaluation methodology incorporates quantitative as well as qualitative assessments on environmental and social impact, economic sustainability, and private sector development impact e.g., demonstration effect.*

Portfolio performance. Comments were made on the varied performance of projects across regions and sectors, particularly the weak performance in Africa. In this regard, one member asked why smaller projects performed badly in comparison to larger projects, and the reasons for poor performance of direct investment and technical assistance to SMEs in Africa. *Management elaborated on the lessons learned in trying to manage small projects in Africa from Washington. In this regard, it said that some changes have been introduced such as using more intermediaries, and increased staffing in Africa through decentralization.*

Concerning the lower evaluated success rates for equity compared to loans, despite the fact that equity has a higher overall contribution to IFC's profitability, one member found it reasonable that higher return was linked to risk-adjusted return; *Management added that the profitability of IFC's equity investment should be looked at on a portfolio basis whereby successful projects drive overall outcome.* Others asked about IFC's criteria, other than customer's demand, for offering equity and loan.

Country approach. Some members stressed the importance of strengthening IFC's country approach taking into account the different needs for private sector development in frontier and nonfrontier countries and markets. In this regard,

few members felt that more could be done to strengthen and institutionalize the CAS. One speaker agreed with IEG's calls for IFC to define roles and priorities in MICs, and whether it should focus on key priority areas affecting the poorest, e.g. infrastructure, and frontier markets. Another proposed a model for looking at a country-level development impact analysis, which may facilitate the analysis of a project and its implications in a particular market. *Management informed that IFC is moving towards a more country-focused strategy under the current decentralization efforts, and when appropriate to programmatic approaches.*

World Bank Group (WBG) synergies. A few members encouraged improving the interaction between the Bank and IFC, including division of labor and consistency of country approaches. One member suggested addressing alignment of incentives and remuneration.

Specific areas for engagement. IFC's focus on rural projects particularly agribusiness and rural microfinance was encouraged. There was also a proposal to focus on climate change and energy efficiency. *Management replied that following IEG's recommendation to place an emphasis on rural development, agribusiness was selected as one of IFC's five priorities, particularly in frontier areas*

Decentralization. There were comments and questions on the cost-effectiveness of decentralization, and the impact on human resources including maintaining adequate staffing, diversity, and incentives to share knowledge while increasing efficiency. Relatedly, one member was concerned about tensions raised during managerial and organizational changes. A speaker cautioned about the use of incentives focused on volume. Others sought further elaboration on the delegation of operational authority to the field, and the quality of supervision of projects. *Management responded that its Industry Departments are working on enhancing knowledge sharing in a decentralized organizational structure, and across the WBG. While noting the* *possibility of higher operational and oversight costs, Management stressed the benefits of decentralization such as closer knowledge of local markets including risks, and empowerment of staff through more delegation. Management informed that it was piloting successfully an incentives system where Bank staff are credited in their annual performance assessment for subnational assets added to IFC book. Management emphasized the importance of using a system that will promote innovation and creativity rather than one focused on a checklist.*

Disclosure of IEG report. Through the full disclosure of the report, IEG expected better accountability. A few speakers welcomed the public disclosure of the report, and the impact on accountability and transparency, which could benefit other multilaterals and private investors, and promote monitoring and evaluation.

Makoto Hosomi, Acting Chairperson

Development Results of IFC-Supported Projects, 1996–2006

T he Independent Evaluation Group of the International Finance Corporation (IEG-IFC) has conducted evaluations of the development results of IFC-supported private sector projects since 1996.[1]

This chapter presents a 10-year retrospective of the development performance of IFC's investment operations and a directional forecast of future results. (IFC did not establish a systematic approach for evaluating project-level results of its advisory operations until 2006.)[2]

Amid considerable variation in private capital flows to emerging markets, IFC has been successful in increasing the level of its investment and advisory services activities in the last 15 years, investing about $50 billion (approximately 4 percent of private capital flows, including funds from cofinanciers). Out of 627 IFC investment operations approved during 1991–2001 that had reached early operating maturity and were evaluated between 1996 and 2006, IFC's year-on-year development success rates (the proportion of IFC-supported projects that achieved high development ratings) have not generally departed greatly from an overall average of 59 percent (65 percent by volume). In the last three years, however, IFC's development success rates have fluctuated significantly—from 58 percent in 2004, to 51 percent in 2005, and to 66 percent in 2006—reflecting industry sector dynamics as well as variations in business climate quality. Continued higher success rates will hinge

on sustained improvements, or nondeterioration, in the business climate quality of emerging market economies as well as improved project risk layering by IFC at approval.

To enable a comprehensive view of IFC's development impact, performance metrics will need to evolve further to capture the wider sector and country-level impacts of IFC-supported projects.

Substantial Increases in IFC Investment and Advisory Services Activities

Private capital flows to developing countries fell in the wake of several crises in the late 1990s, but are again at record levels. Net private capital flows to developing countries grew dramatically between 1991 and 1997, from less than $100 billion per year to about $300 billion per year. Capital flows then fell to under $200 billion in 2002 following various regional and country political and economic crises (including those in Asia in 1998 and Argentina in 2001). Since 2003, private capital flows have again achieved new record levels, reaching $647 billion in 2006, approximately 5 percent of the gross domestic product (GDP) of developing countries. This pattern of growth contrasts sharply with declining official

Figure 1.1. IFC Has Increased Its Private Investment Operations Sixfold since 1991

▶ Since 1991, net private capital flows (of debt and equity) have varied considerably. They rose steadily in 1991–97, before falling back in 1998–2002, and are again at record levels.

The volume of IFC investments has, however, grown almost year-on-year since 1991. IFC was consistent with its mission of moving counter-cyclically to the market during a downturn (1998–2002). IFC investments represent about 1 percent of all private capital flows to developing countries (4 percent, including the funds of cofinanciers), but make up about 30 percent of international finance institution private sector volumes.

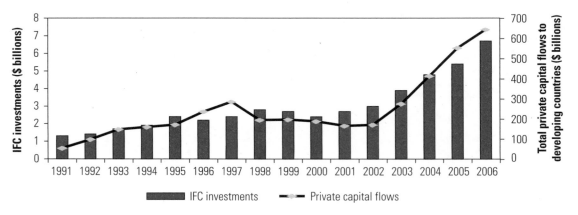

Source: IFC and World Bank databases.

aid to developing country governments. Net official flows (debt plus aid) fell from $78 billion in 1998 to *minus* $5 billion in 2006, reflecting a rising trend in the substitution of official capital in financing for development.[3]

IFC has increased its investment activities sixfold. During 1991–99, IFC's investment commitments almost doubled, with minor dips in 1995 and 1999. Since 1999, IFC has grown its investment operations in every year, with an increase in new investments per year from approximately $2 billion in 1999 to $6 billion in 2006 (figure 1.1). In total, IFC invested about $50 billion in developing countries between 1991 and 2006, a sixfold increase overall. Including funds provided by cofinanciers (IFC normally provides around 25 percent of total project costs), IFC-supported projects have consistently made up about 4 percent of all private capital flows to developing countries. Over the same period, the World Bank provided ap-

Between 1991 and 2006, IFC invested about $50 billion in developing countries.

proximately $340 billion of assistance to the governments of developing countries during this time, with much smaller year-on-year volume changes than those of IFC.[4]

IFC's countercyclical growth during 2000–02 in part reflected the successful implementation of a new growth strategy. The strategy called for a repositioning of IFC ahead of the market on multiple fronts, including leading the private sector into new countries, particularly frontier countries (defined by IFC as being high risk and/or low income, see table 1.1), and sectors (infrastructure, financial markets, and health and education), as well as making a significant push toward second-tier companies and small and medium enterprises (SMEs). A prime example of IFC's countercyclical role was its support for large industrial clients in Turkey through several periods of market turbulence (since the mid-1990s), and their emergence as major engines of economic growth in the country.[5]

IFC has also grown its advisory services operations. The country coverage of active advi-

Table 1.1. IFC Is More Concentrated Than Other Private Capital in Frontier Countries

▶ If a country meets the criteria of being high risk (with an Institutional Investor Country Credit Rating of less than 30) and/or low income (gross national income of less than $826 per capita),[6] then IFC classifies it as a frontier country. As the table below shows, frontier countries accounted for about 15 percent of developing country GDP in 2005. In line with its strategy, IFC has a far higher share of the commitments in these countries relative to foreign direct investment.

Risk and income level	Examples[a]	IFC classification	Share of developing country GDP (2005)	Share of developing country foreign direct investment (2005)	Share of IFC commitments (2006)
High risk and/or low income	Bangladesh; India; Nigeria; Pakistan; Vietnam	Frontier	15%	12% (ratio to GDP share of 0.8)	29% (ratio to GDP share of 1.9)
Neither high risk nor low income	Brazil; China; Mexico; Russia; Turkey	Nonfrontier	85%	88% (ratio to GDP share of 1.0)	71% (ratio to GDP share of 0.9)

Sources: IEG, derived from IFC documentation and databases; and the Institutional Investor.

a. In the each case, the country examples are those with the five largest economies (measured by GDP) in 2005.

sory services operations has increased from 72 in 1996, to 134 in 2005, with frontier countries accounting for the majority of new advisory services commitments. The volume of advisory services commitments has, accordingly, increased from about $53 million per year in 1996, to $222 million in 2005.[7]

Most IFC-Supported Projects Achieved High Development Ratings

IEG[8] evaluates the development and investment performance of IFC's operations. Each year, IEG-IFC assesses the performance of a random sample of IFC's investment and advisory services operations (see appendix A), as a way to provide accountability for the performance of IFC operations and to identify lessons that will inform future strategy and operations (box 1.1). As such, IEG-IFC assesses the development and IFC investment results arising from individual projects, and synthesizes performance at the sector, thematic, country, regional, and global levels to present aggregate accounts of IFC's development impacts (or effectiveness). There are, however, accordant limitations in the inferences one can

draw about the wider development impacts of IFC. This is partly because of the difficulty in attributing project-level impacts to wider development in a country and the often indirect nature by which IFC operations help promote private sector development and contribute to the reduction of poverty (see figure 1.2).

Fifty-nine percent of operations (65 percent by volume) achieved high development ratings. On average, based on a random sample of 627 operations, 59 percent of IFC-supported projects between 1996 and 2006 achieved high development ratings (65 percent when weighted by the size of IFC's investment in each case). The project development rating is a synthesis of four subindicators: project business success; economic sustainability; environmental and social effects; and impact on private sector development. These indicators are explored in more detail in box 1.1; box 1.2 illustrates how the indicators describe successful and less successful IFC-supported projects. Development ratings are higher by volume because larger operations tend to be more successful than smaller operations.

Box 1.1. IEG Independently Rates the Development and Investment Performance of IFC Operations

Each year, IEG-IFC independently assesses the development results of a random sample of IFC's investment and advisory services operations, as a way to provide accountability for past performance and to identify lessons that will inform IFC and World Bank Group strategy and operations going forward. IEG is independent in reporting directly to the Board of Directors of the World Bank Group rather than to IFC Management.

IEG-IFC carries out two types of evaluations—micro and macro evaluations. **Micro evaluations** are assessments of the performance of individual IFC investment and advisory services operations, which are first self-evaluated by IFC staff before being validated by IEG-IFC. Micro evaluations provide the building blocks for macro evaluations of sector, country, regional, and global performance, or on a theme, such as IFC's experiences with small and medium enterprises. **Macro evaluations** link project-level outcomes to prevailing country and regional conditions, as well as internal factors, such as the way IFC organizes itself and its work processes and procedures.

The timing of an evaluation depends on its nature. For investment operations, IEG-IFC evaluates project performance at "early operating maturity" (usually 18 months into commercial operations, which is generally five years after approval), while for advisory services operations, the evaluation is carried out after the project closes. Macro evaluations are often carried out to tie in with IEG-World Bank evaluations of the same sectors, countries, or regions, but such evaluations also address issues specific to IFC's operations and strategic priorities.

All evaluations look at the development results, as well as the investment success (in the case of investment operations) of IFC's operations. The project **development rating** is a bottom-line assessment of the project's results across four development dimensions, relative to what would have occurred without the project.[9] Operations are judged to be at least satisfactory based on the following criteria.

- *Project business success.* For real-sector projects, operations generated a project financial rate of return at least equal to the company's cost of capital (inclusive of a 350-basis-point spread to its equity investors over its lenders' nominal yield); for financial sector projects, the associated subportfolios or asset growth

contributed positively to the intermediary's profitability, financial condition, and business objectives.
- *Economic sustainability.* Where measurable, operations generated an economic rate of return of at least 10 percent. This indicator takes into account net gains or losses by nonfinanciers, unquantifiable impacts, and contributions to widely held development objectives.
- *Environmental and social effects.* Operations met or exceeded IFC's environmental, social, health, and safety requirements at approval, and (since 1998) Bank Group policies and guidelines, as well as local standards that would apply if the project were appraised today.
- *Private sector development impacts.* Whether a project's private sector development impact beyond the project is positive, particularly its demonstration effect, in creating a sustainable enterprise capable of attracting finance, increasing competition, and establishing linkages.

IFC's **investment rating** is an assessment of the gross profit contribution quality of an IFC loan and/or equity investment, that is, without taking into account transaction costs or the cost of IFC equity capital.

- *Loan.* Loans are rated satisfactory provided they are expected to be repaid in full with interest and fees as scheduled (or are prepaid or rescheduled without loss).
- *Equity.* Equities are rated satisfactory if they yield an appropriate premium on the return on a loan to the same company (a nominal, dollar, internal rate of return greater than or equal to the fixed loan interest rate,[10] plus a premium).

Unlike other development financial institutions that focus on the public sector, IFC's private sector projects face competition and, therefore, the evaluation framework for investment operations captures the inherent commercial risks and market factors affecting the projects. Accordingly, results cannot be directly compared with those of public sector institutions such as the World Bank, which employ different evaluation approaches, including in terms of focus, timing of evaluation, and benchmarks used[11] (see box 1.4 and appendix A).

There has been some variability in the development subindicators. IFC operations have done better in terms of private sector development impacts beyond the project, environmental and so-

cial effects, and economic sustainability (all were above the synthesis success rate of 59 percent between 1996 and 2006, see table 1.2). IFC operations have done less well in terms of project business suc-

Figure 1.2. IFC Operations Can Help Reduce Poverty through a Chain of Events

▶ IFC activities can help to reduce poverty via a sequence of steps. For instance, an investment operation can have positive demonstration effects, leading to a number of companies entering a market, thus creating jobs and economic growth, which ultimately helps to reduce poverty among workers and consumers alike (on the basis that prices fall and/or quality improves with increased competition).

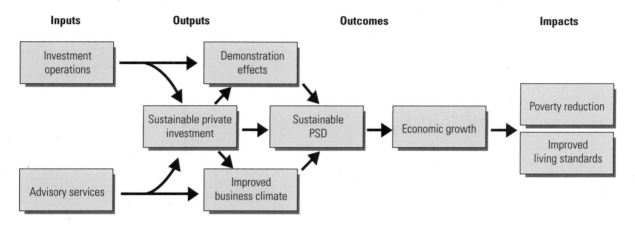

Source: IEG.

Box 1.2. Examples of Successful and Less Successful IFC Projects

Successful project: The project was the installation of a new digital cellular network in an Asian country, to provide 55 percent coverage by area and increase access to telephone services among poor rural communities. At the start time of the project, the country had one of the lowest telephone density rates in the world and a wait time of more than 10 years for a fixed telephone line. The project was a major commercial success (an excellent project business-success rating), with a subscriber base of nearly half a million, more than twice what was anticipated. Economic sustainability was rated as excellent because the project yielded outstanding returns to the economy, including taxes and duties paid to the government, revenue-sharing payments to the regulator, license fees, and lease payments to a railway company for using its fiber-optic backbone. Environmental and social effects were rated as satisfactory, with the company committed to sound environmental and social performance, in compliance with World Bank Group guidelines. Private sector development impacts were excellent, with the project increasing cellular competition, and resulting in lower tariffs, increased range, and improved quality for users, as well as improving the essential infrastructure for other private sector development.

Less successful project: The project was a pilot credit agency line serving wood processors and furniture manufacturers in a post-conflict transition economy in Europe. The companies were previously part of a state-owned conglomerate which collapsed. Project business success was unsatisfactory because all of the companies financed through the agency line fell into financial distress. IFC provided technical assistance to build management capacity (ahead of a planned privatization) but it was insufficient to bridge their lack of expertise, and problems were compounded by difficult trading conditions. Economic sustainability was also unsatisfactory because none of the companies had proved to be a sustainable source of employment, tax revenues, or added value. Their expected contribution to postwar reconstruction was limited. Environmental and social effects were unsatisfactory because the companies did not meet the prescribed standards, with one furniture manufacturer polluting local air quality, soil, and surface and ground waters. Finally, private sector development impacts were unsatisfactory because no privatization occurred due to a lack of interest from domestic and foreign investors. Moreover, the agency line failed in its objective to help build expertise within the agent banks to support future private enterprise in the country.

Table 1.2. Most IFC-Supported Projects Achieved High Development Ratings, 1996–2006

▶ Most IFC-supported projects were, on balance, delivering (and were expected to deliver in the long run) sustainable development across the four dimensions that IEG rates: their financial, economic, environmental and social performance, as well as their contribution to private sector development beyond the project (see box 1.1 for more details on the criteria used to rate each dimension, and box 1.4 on the general noncomparability of these results with those of other institutions such as the World Bank).

IFC projects have performed better, in terms of private sector development impacts beyond the project, environmental and social effects, and economic sustainability—all were above the overall rating of 59 percent. IFC projects have done less well in terms of project business success (46 percent by number, 50 percent by volume), which reduces the overall development rating. Weaker performance on project business success is mainly due to the inherent commercial risk of a private sector business—IFC projects face the test of market competition—combined with business climate risk. However, some businesses that achieve only marginal commercial performance (they achieve a positive return but fail to achieve the satisfactory financial rate of return "hurdle rate") can still operate in an economically sustainable manner, and have positive environmental and social effects and private sector development impacts.

Success rates are higher by volume because larger operations tend to be more successful than smaller operations.

Development Indicator	Percentage with high development ratings, by number	Percentage with high development ratings, weighted by commitment volume
Overall development rating		
(a bottom-line assessment of the below indicators)	59	65
(i) Project business success	46	50
(ii) Economic sustainability	62	65
(iii) Environmental and social effects	67	72
(iv) Private sector development impact (beyond the project)	72	76

Source: IEG.

Note: Performance reported above is based on the evaluations of 627 projects between 1996 and 2006.

cess (46 percent by number, 50 percent by volume), reflecting in large part the inherent commercial risk of a private sector business. However, even some businesses that achieve only marginal commercial performance, can still operate in an economically sustainable manner, and have positive environmental and social effects and private sector development impacts. Environmental and social effects ratings for IFC-supported projects have varied in the past decade due to the introduction of stricter requirements,[12] the examination of a growing number of issues in environmental and social assessments and evaluations, and the varying complexity and industry sectors of evaluated projects. Appendix B provides trend information for each indicator.

Development performance is assessed across four dimensions.

Performance has also differed across regions and sectors. By region, project development results have been weaker in Africa, driven by persistently high-risk business climates, together with below-average IFC work quality, the willingness by IFC to take greater project risks in the region, and below-average project environmental and social compliance. By sector, IFC-supported projects in the infrastructure and the extractive sectors have achieved better development performance, with more mixed results in general manufacturing and services, funds, and health and education operations. Chapter 2 discusses regional and sector performance variations in more detail, in the context of what we have learned about private sector development in the last decade.

Performance has fluctuated substantially in the last three years. Previous IEG reviews of IFC's development results have focused on the development performance of IFC-supported projects that were evaluated in the most recent three years, to ensure their relevance for informing IFC strategy and operations going forward. While this review, overall, adopts a longer-term perspective, this section addresses the quality of IFC's development results since 2004. Figure 1.3 shows that project development ratings have varied substantially, from 58 percent in 2004, to 52 percent in 2005, and to 66 percent in 2006.

Recent variations in project development results in part reflect sectoral specifics. The fall in the proportion of projects with high development ratings, from 58 percent in 2004, to 52 percent in 2005, coincided with the start of IFC's frontier growth strategy and with significant organizational changes. In pursuit of its frontier growth strategy, IFC faced new risks in its operations, with investments in new countries[13] and in new sectors. For example, a Health and Education Department was created in 2000, and the number of investments in the social sectors peaked around that time. These investments—approved in 2000 and evaluated in 2005—while

small in number, exhibit lower success rates than investments in other sectors. That time also coincided with the technology and Internet bubble, and in line with the high-risk nature of that sector, few of IFC's investments in Internet firms proved to be successful.[14] IFC's investments in general manufacturing also did not fare well, compared with the all-sector average or compared with general manufacturing investments by IFC historically, in part due to increased competition between IFC-supported operations and Chinese producers.

Factors outside of IFC's control also contributed to development impact quality. There were a number of political and economic crises in the emerging markets before and during 2000 (including the after-effects of the Asian crisis in 1998). The country risk ratings for 37 percent of projects approved in non-high-risk countries actually deteriorated to high risk after project approval, while the country risk ratings for 79 percent of high-risk approvals remained high risk. As previous evaluations have shown, deterioration in a country's business climate risk adversely affects the development performance of projects in that country. By contrast, most operations evaluated in

IFC projects face the test of market competition.

Figure 1.3. Trends in Project Development Performance, 1996–2006

▶ Based on 627 evaluations of IFC-supported projects between 1996 and 2006, 59 percent achieved high development ratings. Performance was above average between 1996 and 1998, below average in 2005, and then above average in 2006.

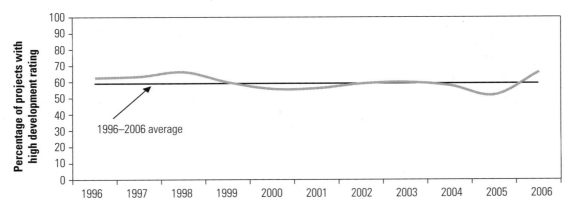

Source: IEG.

2006 benefited from the fact that their host countries achieved a significant improvement in business climate risk after approval. This helped boost companies' business success and economic sustainability in particular.

Further Improvement Is Anticipated

Project high-risk intensity affects development performance. The projects that IFC supports, by their nature, typically face intrinsic business risks. To an extent, IFC can control the level of project risk, first by screening out projects with unmanageable risks, and for projects processed through to approval, mitigating risks through appropriate project and investment structuring. IEG has found that, in aggregate, high levels of risk can detract from the quality of a project's development impact. As figure 1.4 shows, projects with more high-risk factors present achieve lower development ratings, with the presence of four or more high-risk factors generally equating to lower-than-average development success. For projects approved since 2002, there is no independently validated evaluation data because these projects have not yet reached early

IFC can control the level of project risk.

operating maturity. In the absence of ex-post information, IEG analyzes the level of project risk in recent commitments to provide an ex-ante, directional indication of the trend in future success rates. IEG screens projects for eight risk factors: sponsor quality, market risk, debt service burden, project type, sector risk, country business climate at approval, IFC credit review intensity, and non-repeat-project risk. Appendix A describes IEG's methodology and each risk factor in further detail.

The high-risk intensity of IFC projects at approval has fallen. Fifty-nine percent of projects evaluated between 1995 and 2000 carried four or more high-risk factors, compared with 46 percent between 2002 and 2005.[15] This pattern reflects a declining trend almost year-on-year since 1995.[16] The decrease in high-risk layering is likely a result of various quality-enhancement steps taken by IFC since 1998. IFC has made a number of organizational changes, such as the creation of a Credit Department, portfolio units, equity desks, and deploying more investment staff in the field, as well as several procedural changes that have increased the rigor of front-end review, facilitated

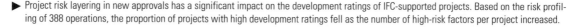

Figure 1.4. Projects with More High-Risk Factors Achieve Lower Development Ratings

▶ Project risk layering in new approvals has a significant impact on the development ratings of IFC-supported projects. Based on the risk profiling of 388 operations, the proportion of projects with high development ratings fell as the number of high-risk factors per project increased.

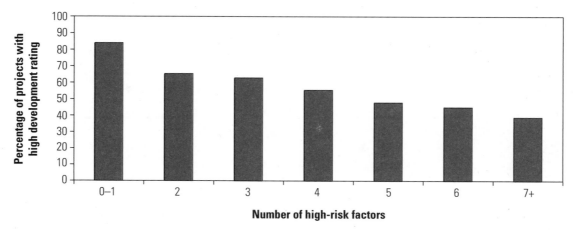

Source: IEG.

Note: IFC investment success rates have a similar relationship with the number of high-risk factors, although the dropoff in success rates with four or more high-risk factors is even sharper for investment success rates than it is for development success rates.

▶ The level of country business-climate risk following project approval has a large impact on project development ratings. Where business climate risk is improving, IFC-supported projects are more likely to be successful, whereas when business climate quality is deteriorating, projects are less likely to be successful.

Among operations being evaluated in 2007, the positive shift in average business climate risk that they have faced since project approval (measured by changes in Institutional Investor Country Credit ratings and weighted according to the evaluation sample) is the greatest it has been since the current evaluation system was introduced in 1996. Accordingly, it is reasonable to expect IFC-supported projects to achieve higher development ratings in 2007.

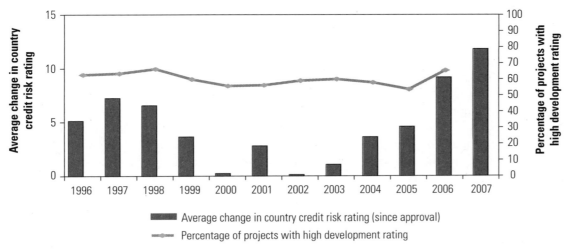

Average change in country credit risk rating (since approval)

Percentage of projects with high development rating

Sources: IEG and Institutional Investor.

Note: The development performance of the 2007 cohort of projects is currently being evaluated.

closer portfolio management, and strengthened environmental appraisal of real-sector projects. Accordingly, the share of new operations with high review risk and financial structuring risk fell sharply between periods 1995–2000 and 2002–05. Assuming IEG's risk profiling retains its predictive capability, other things being equal, this trend in project high-risk intensity bodes well for IFC project development results in the coming years.

Even with high-risk intensity, IFC may be able to achieve sound development results. The development performance of projects supported through recently approved IFC investments will also hinge on the quality of IFC structuring, appraisal, supervision, and its role and contribution. This is illustrated in the fact that with high work quality (good structuring, appraisal, supervision, and IFC role and contribution), evaluated IFC projects with four or more high-risk

factors achieved high development impact quality 77 percent of the time. In those cases, IFC was able to effectively manage high project risks to deliver high development results.

Sustained higher development success rates are anticipated in 2007, due to improved business climate risk. As reported above, IEG has found that improving business climate conditions between project approval and evaluation increase development impact quality. In recent years, the business climates of many countries in which IFC is active have improved considerably. In addition to the 25 countries that have graduated from the high-risk group since 2001, within the 2007 evaluation sample (as yet to be evaluated ex post), the level of positive change in country risk ratings is unprecedented (figure 1.5).[17] Early indications of how the business climate risk profiles of the 2008 evaluation sample will look are also positive.[18] Combined with better risk mitigation at approval, we can reasonably expect that the above-average development performance observed in 2006 will likely be sustained in 2007.

With higher investment volumes, IFC's development impact ought to increase commensurately in the coming years. Given higher investment volumes, with commitments increasing twofold from $3 billion per year in 2001 to $6 billion per year in 2006, and expectations of further significant increases over the coming years, IFC's corporate development footprint should expand commensurately. This expectation rests on two key assumptions. First, the business climate risk in the countries in which IFC is investing will continue, on average, to improve. It remains too early to predict the impact of business climate changes on post-2004 IFC investment approvals, because these will not reach early operating maturity (and hence not be eligible for full evaluation) for three or more years. Second, as in the past, the development impact quality of IFC-supported projects will, in the future, hinge on factors internal to IFC, such as how effective IFC is in increasing its field presence, maintaining transaction quality and ensuring that lessons from past operations are internalized (which is to say that IFC repeats successes that can be replicated, and avoids past mistakes). Some of the issues raised by IFC's efforts at greater decentralization are explored further in chapter 3.

No Trade-off between Development Results and IFC Investment Returns

Between 1996 and 2006, 46 percent of evaluated projects achieved both high development and investment ratings. Considering development results alongside IFC investment returns, out of the 627 projects evaluated between 1996 and 2006, 46 percent achieved *high-high* results (high development success as well as high IFC investment return, as defined in box 1.1). Meanwhile, 31 percent delivered *low-low* results (low development success as well as low IFC investment return). By volume of commitments, some 53 percent of projects achieved *high-high* results, while 26 percent delivered *low-low* results (figure 1.6). This pattern of performance has strengthened

over time, with an increase in *high-high* results implying improved project execution by IFC. The relationship is robust among three of the four component development indicators and IFC investment success: project business success, economic sustainability, and private sector development (PSD) impacts, but not environmental and social effects (with effective environmental and social performance typically still being achieved when IFC's investment return is low).[19]

IFC has not actively supported projects where there was a trade-off between profitability and development results. Only 23 percent of the 627 evaluated operations had mixed results (high development success with low investment success in 13 percent of cases; low development success and high investment success in 10 percent of cases). Consequently, it is apparent that there is not a necessary trade-off between development results and IFC investment returns and that IFC has not consciously supported projects where there was likely to be a trade-off between these two dimensions. Projects failed to achieve *high-high* ratings for a number of reasons. These include the inherent commercial risk in different industry sectors, adverse business climates, poor sponsor quality, or shortfalls in IFC work quality. Of the 23 percent that achieved mixed results, IFC's choice of financing instrument was the most common reason. Proportionately, more operations involving equity achieved high development success and low investment returns (some four-fifths of these cases), while more operations involving loans achieved low development success and high investment returns (in about nine-tenths of the cases), for reasons described below. As appendix B shows, loans featuring high IFC work quality are the most likely combination to achieve *high-high* ratings.

Loans have been more likely than equity instruments to achieve high (above benchmark) investment ratings but, in aggregate, IFC has achieved higher returns from its equity portfolio. Considered individually, loans have a higher chance of performing successfully than equity investments (see table 1.3), reflecting the different inherent risks of each instrument. In the case of

Figure 1.6. IFC-Supported Projects Show No Trade-off between Development Results and IFC Investment Returns

▶ Of the IFC operations evaluated between 1996 and 2006, about three-quarters (by number and volume) resulted in *high-high* ratings (high development result/high IFC investment return) or *low-low* ratings (low development result/low IFC investment return). For the most part, therefore, IFC has not supported projects where there was an apparent trade-off between development results and investment returns. Where project development results and IFC investment returns were not correlated (23 percent of cases), proportionately more operations involving equity achieved high development success and low investment returns (square 2), while more operations involving loans achieved low development success and high investment returns (square 3), reflecting different investment risk associated with each instrument.

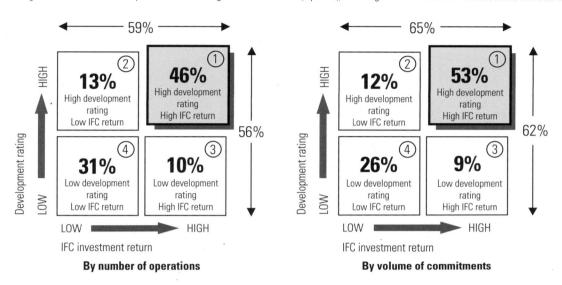

Source: IEG.

loans, IFC has a ranking claim on company cash-flow for loan service as well as the collateral security package, which together provide some downside protection. Equity investments, however, must meet rigorous return standards to compensate for the instrument's subordination and currency risk. Accordingly, while 68 percent of equity investments generated a positive return, only 31 percent achieved high (above benchmark) investment ratings. In aggregate, IFC has been rewarded with higher returns on its portfolio of equity investments in recent years. In common with all commercial equity portfolios, the few successful investments tend to be major contributors to overall profitability. In IFC's case, its equity investments in Africa have recently helped IFC's portfolio of investment operations in the region become profitable (after losses each year during the 1990s). Equity investments, in general, have made a significant contribution to IFC's retained earnings and hence its capacity to scale up the volume of its investment and advisory services op-

erations in recent years. Maintaining this level of profitability will, however, depend on continued investor optimism in the emerging markets and consequent high valuations—particularly given the high ratio of unrealized to realized gains (about a 4:1 ratio). Appendix B provides further details on the profitability of IFC's whole portfolio of investment operations.

IFC has achieved higher returns from its equity portfolio.

Comprehensive Evaluation of IFC's Development Effectiveness Remains a Major Challenge

Substantial progress has been made in measuring project development results, but challenges remain. IFC has increased the breadth and depth of its monitoring and self-evaluation systems, such that IFC is now tracking its development results across its portfolio of investment and advisory operations. Preliminary

Table 1.3. More Loan Than Equity Operations Achieved High Investment Ratings

▶ Loans are more than twice as likely as equity operations to achieve high investment ratings, due to the different inherent risk involved in each instrument. In the case of loans, IFC has a ranking claim on company cashflow for loan service and the collateral security package that together provide some downside protection. Equity investments, however, must meet rigorous return standards to compensate for the instrument's sub-ordination and currency risk. Accordingly, while 68 percent of equity investments generated a positive return, only 31 percent achieved high (above benchmark) investment ratings. In aggregate, however, IFC has been rewarded with higher returns on its portfolio basis of equity investments in recent years (see appendix B).

Instrument	Number of operations	Percentage of operations with high ratings, by number	Percentage of operations with high ratings, by commitment volume	Percentage of equity operations with positive returns (real internal rate of return >0)
All instruments, 1996–2006	627[a]	56	62	
Loans, 1996–2006	473	74	78	
Equity investments, 1996–2006	329	31	30	68 (70 by volume)

Source: IEG.

a. Some operations involved a combination of loan and equity instruments. The total number of operations is, therefore, not a straight sum of the number of loan and equity operations.

data are emerging under the Development Outcome Tracking System (DOTS), and IEG will report in next year's *Independent Evaluation of IFC's Development Results* on its validation of this data. Building on the above progress, IFC could advance its metrics to better capture the wider impacts of its operations, including those covering broader environmental and social effects, as well as undertaking more rigorous impact evaluation, to get a better understanding of its true development footprint (box 1.3).

Comparing the development performance of IFC-supported projects with those of other development organizations is problematic.
A Multilateral Development Bank Evaluation Cooperation Group was established in 1996, with the aim of harmonizing evaluation standards among development banks. Based on a January 2005 benchmarking report by an independent consultant of the Evaluation Cooperation Group, IFC's standards are currently closely aligned with the harmonized standards, while other institutions

are still in the process of implementing these standards. Although substantial progress toward harmonization of private sector evaluation approaches has been made, continued differences mean that IFC's results are not yet comparable to those of other international financial institutions. These differences generally reflect different organizational mandates and objectives and varying degrees of adoption of the standards.[20] For example, while the European Bank for Reconstruction and Development (EBRD) focuses on assisting countries in their transition process, the World Bank Group tasks itself with poverty reduction and sustainable private sector development (and even within the Bank Group there are differences; see box 1.4).

There is some degree of comparability with EBRD on one subindicator.
Despite differences in operational mandates, IFC's private sector development impact rating (one of the four components of the synthesis development impact rating) is somewhat comparable to EBRD's "tran-

Box 1.3. IFC Is Deepening Its Development Results Measurement but Methodological Challenges Remain

IFC Has Introduced a New Development Outcome Tracking System for All Investment Operations

In July 2005, IFC established a new Development Effectiveness Unit within the office of the Chief Economist. The unit seeks to systematically track IFC's development results for all investment projects throughout their life cycles. To perform this work, the unit employs the Development Outcome Tracking System (DOTS), which is distinct from IFC's existing monitoring and self-evaluation system—the Expanded Project Supervision Report (XPSR) system—in that DOTS:

- Examines potential development effectiveness before early operating maturity;
- Does not assess IFC's work quality;
- Currently covers the whole population of active investment operations (the XPSR system covers a random sample of both closed and active operations), although in future, DOTS ratings will also be available for closed projects; and
- Updates development ratings with each new Project Supervision Report (whereas the XPSR system assesses performance once, at early operating maturity).

The two systems are expected to complement, rather than compete with one another. The first full results arising from DOTS (preliminary results were announced in November 2006)[21] are expected to be announced publicly in October 2007.

IFC Is Also Piloting a Monitoring and Self-Evaluation System for Its Advisory Services Operations

Since 2006, IFC has been piloting a monitoring and self-evaluation system, a DOTS for advisory services, which tracks the development results arising from advisory services projects. The results of these pilots are also expected to be included in IFC's annual report. Appendix A contains further details on the methodology IFC employs to measures its development results in this area.

A Key Challenge Is to Capture the Wider Sector and Country-Level Impacts of IFC-Supported Projects

While these are steps forward in the monitoring and evaluation of IFC's development effectiveness, they will not completely capture the full development impacts of IFC's activities. For example, these systems will not always pick up the wider, non-project-level effects of IFC's operations, such as the impact on energy efficiency in a sector or country from a series of power sector investments.

Time Will Tell Whether the Development Results Identified through DOTS Are Reliable

Because DOTS assigns ratings before operating maturity (when operational performance tends to stabilize, according to the trend in IFC's own project credit ratings, as well as an assessment of the stability of equity ratings postevaluation),[22] anticipated results from recently approved operations will need to be treated with caution. DOTS ratings assigned to operations that IEG has already evaluated are similar to the ratings reported by IEG, which is not surprising because these operations have reached early operating maturity and therefore their performance has stabilized. It remains to be seen whether ratings assigned under DOTS to projects not yet operationally mature (and not yet validated by IEG) are reliable.

---

sition impact." Based on 2000–05 evaluations, EBRD's "transition impact" success rate was approximately the same as IFC's PSD success rate in EBRD countries over the same period (see figure 1.7). Nonetheless, there is no common basis for benchmarking the overall development effectiveness of the two institutions.[23] Slightly different timings for evaluation (EBRD evaluates performance after 12 months of operations while IFC evaluates performance after 18 months of operations) and hurdle rates for effective performance (for example, in determining what constitutes a satisfactory investment rating) may also have an impact on results comparability.[24]

Box 1.4. IFC and World Bank Development Results Are Generally Not Comparable

A Shared Mission to Reduce Poverty . . . but Different Means and Clients to Deliver on This Mission

The World Bank—which is comprised of the International Bank for Reconstruction and Development, and the International Development Association—IFC, and the Multilateral Investment Guarantee Agency all work to promote sustainable economic growth and poverty reduction.

In pursuing the goal of sustainable economic growth and poverty reduction, each institution uses different mechanisms and structures to reach its often distinct clients. For example, while the Bank provides loans and advisory services to governments for various development purposes, IFC invests in, and provides technical assistance to, private sector companies. Sometimes, IFC does work with governments directly, for instance, in seeking to improve the ease of doing business or in facilitating municipal finance, but most often its clients are private sector companies.

Different types of development engagement are also associated with different levels of risk (including the risk of market competition in IFC's case), as well as different timescales and accountabilities. Each institution has historically organized itself along different lines, the Bank by country and regional teams, and IFC by industry department and region.

IFC Projects Are Assessed against Market Parameters

In the Bank, evaluation systems assess how the results of the Bank's development interventions with governments measure up against their own stated objectives. At the project level, this methodology focuses on relevance, efficacy, efficiency, sustainability, and institutional development impact of Bank operations.[25] IFC evaluations, however, assess IFC's development performance in terms of whether the projects IFC supports achieve project business success, economic sustainability, positive environmental and social effects, and beneficial private sector development impacts beyond the project. Unlike Bank projects, IFC-supported projects are assessed against market parameters and face market competition once they are operational. Given the close link between investment and development results, this may have a consequence for their ability, relative to Bank projects, to achieve high development ratings. Finally, IFC evaluations are carried out at early operating maturing, typically 18 months into operations, which is approximately 5 years after project approval, rather than at project close, as with Bank operations. Appendix A provides a more detailed comparison of the different evaluation approaches employed by the two institutions.

Possible Comparability of Performance in Advisory Services

IFC is now starting to systematically monitor and evaluate the effectiveness of its advisory services operations (see box 1.3). Because IFC's approach in evaluating its advisory services is relatively similar to that used by the Bank for its own advisory services, there may be the potential for a comparison of success rates, especially where both institutions are working with governments.

Figure 1.7. EBRD and IFC Achieved Similar Development Ratings on One Subindicator

▶ While not comparable in overall terms, there is some degree of comparability between the development performance of IFC and EBRD on one specific subindicator. IFC's private sector development impact rating (one of four subcomponents of the synthesis development impact rating) can generally be compared to EBRD's "transition impact" ratings.

Looking at the period 2000–05, for the countries in which both EBRD and IFC have operations, IFC's private sector development impact rating was below that of EBRD's transition impact rating in three years (2000, 2003, and 2004); above it in two years (2001 and 2002); and about the same in 2005.

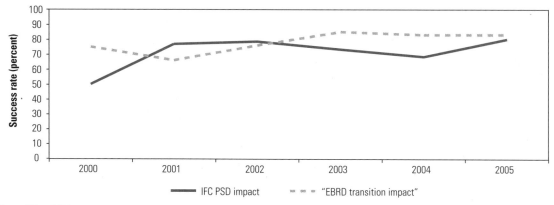

Source: IEG and EBRD.

Note: EBRD typically evaluates performance after 12 months of operations, while IFC evaluates performance after 18 months of operations.

Lessons from 10 Years of Private Sector Development Evaluation

This is IEG's tenth annual review of the development results of IFC-supported projects, a good point at which to take stock of what evaluation findings tell us about the conditions for effective private sector development. A decade of evaluation[1] has revealed five key drivers of IFC's project development results, most notably, IFC's work quality throughout the project cycle.

Development Results Are Driven by Five Factors

From 10 years of PSD evaluation, IEG has identified five factors that have a significant impact on a project's development results:

A. Changes in the quality of a country's business climate following project approval;
B. Type of industry sector;
C. Quality of the sponsor;
D. Level of product market, client company, and project type risks; and
E. IFC work quality.

Taken together, these factors successfully explain the development performance of about two-thirds of IFC-supported projects. Appendix A provides details on the statistical significance of individual factors, as well as their subcomponents, in predicting IFC project development results.

A. Changes in the Quality of a Country's Business Climate Following Project Approval

Business climate quality materially affects levels of private investment, as the contrasting experiences of Asia and Africa illustrate. As discussed earlier in the report, the overall pattern among developing countries in recent years is one of improving business climate risk—as proxied by changes in the *Institutional Investor* Country Credit Risk ratings of these countries. There is, nonetheless, considerable variation by region. As figure 2.1 shows, the East Asia and Pacific Region has had better country risk ratings than other regions. Other regions, particularly Europe and Central Asia, have "caught up," except for Africa, which has improved little since 1996. This variation has had a material impact on the level of private investment in each region (see figure 2.2). Africa not only has the lowest proportion of private

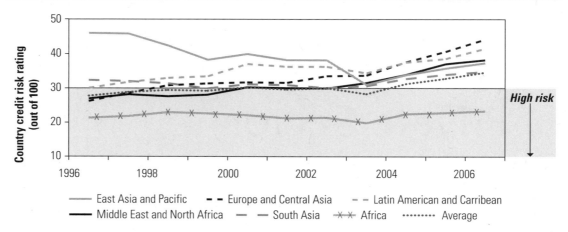

Figure 2.1. Much Riskier Business Climates in Africa, with Some Improvement since 2003

Source: Institutional Investor.

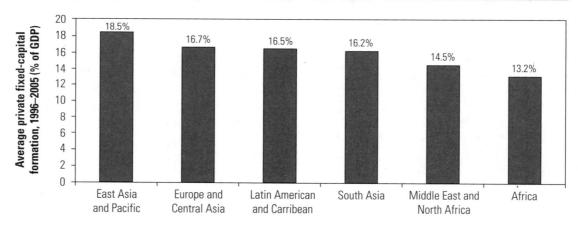

Figure 2.2. Much Lower Private Investment in Africa Than Elsewhere

Source: World Bank Group, Global Development Finance database.

investment relative to gross domestic product (GDP), but also by far the lowest in monetary terms because African GDP is much lower than the GDP of other regions.

In the last 10 years, IFC has been active in difficult business environments. Thirty-seven percent of IFC's 1997 commitments (the year before the frontier strategy was articulated) were in low-income and/or high-risk countries. In 2006, this proportion was 29 percent, which reflected the graduation of a number of large economies (including China and Russia) to nonfrontier status, but also shows that IFC has successfully pursued investments in frontier countries against a decline in their share of GDP (from 40 percent to 15 percent) and a dearth of capital inflows (as proxied by their low share of foreign direct in-

Table 2.1. IFC Success Rates Are Significantly Better Where Country Business Climate Risk Is Improving, or Not Deteriorating

▶ IFC has been approximately 20 percentage points more successful, in development and investment terms, where the business climate risk in the country in which the operation is taking place has improved from high risk to non–high risk. Conversely, where business climate quality has worsened from non–high risk to high risk, IFC has been roughly 25 percentage points less successful.

Change in country business-climate risk postentry	Number of operations	Percentage of projects with high development ratings	Percentage of projects with high investment ratings
Improved from high risk	102	75	72
Stayed high risk	168	54	51
Stayed non–high risk	216	60	56
Deteriorated from non–high risk to high risk	40	35	33

Source: IEG, based on Institutional Investor country credit risk ratings.

vestment). If IFC's commitments in frontier regions within its top 10 middle-income countries (MICs) are included, the frontier share of commitments increases to 38 percent.

Where a country's business climate risk has improved following project approval, development performance has been better. Projects in high-risk business climates are typically exposed to macroeconomic instability, weak physical and financial infrastructure, cumbersome regulatory burdens, and high levels of corruption and informality. It is not surprising, therefore, that improvements in these attributes have a beneficial effect on IFC investments and, by extension, on private sector development more widely in a country. In fact, IFC has been approximately 20 percentage points more successful, in development and investment terms, where the business climate risk in the country in which the operation is taking place has improved from high risk to non-high risk between approval and evaluation (see table 2.1). The potential for business climate improvement is, of course, particularly great in conflict-affected countries, and project evaluations show that IFC can achieve high development ratings even from such weak starting points in terms of country investment

risk.[2] Conversely, where business climate quality deteriorated during the life of a project, ratings were 25 percentage points lower.

It is accordingly crucial that IFC work closely with partners to help sustain the trend of improving business climates. IFC carries out many activities to help improve business climates, such as investment financing for demonstration effects, technical assistance to the public sector on legal and regulatory issues, and advisory assistance to the private sector for capacity building.[3] Nonetheless, bringing about improvements in the business climate to enable successful private sector growth needs the help of governments and other development partners to be successful. The extent of IFC–World Bank cooperation in this direction is discussed in chapter 3.

B. Type of Industry Sector
IFC-supported projects have achieved better development results in infrastructure, extractive sectors, and financial markets. As illustrated in figure 2.3, IFC has achieved above-average development performance in infrastructure projects (78 percent), which, by their nature, have provided large economic benefits and positive externalities (see Brazil transport examples in box 2.1), and in extractive industry operations

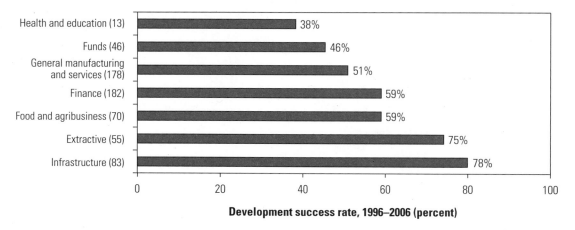

Figure 2.3. IFC Development Ratings Varied Considerably by Industry Department

▶ Based on 627 projects evaluated between 1996 and 2006, IFC has achieved the best development results in its infrastructure projects (78 percent). IFC has also achieved above-average success rates in the extractive industries (74 percent) and in financial markets projects outside of Africa (63 percent, not shown).

On the other hand, IFC has achieved lower development results in the funds (46 percent), and general manufacturing and services sectors (51 percent). Health and education projects also show below-average ratings, although only 13 projects have been evaluated to date, and these are relatively new sectors for IFC.

Health and education (13) — 38%
Funds (46) — 46%
General manufacturing and services (178) — 51%
Finance (182) — 59%
Food and agribusiness (70) — 59%
Extractive (55) — 75%
Infrastructure (83) — 78%

Development success rate, 1996–2006 (percent)

Source: IEG.

Note: Numbers in parentheses refer to the number of evaluated projects; Infrastructure classification includes Information Communications Technology projects as well as transport and utilities projects.

(75 percent). The overall success rate of financial sector operations was the same as the all-sector average of 59 percent over the last decade, although this success rate was depressed by below-average performance in Africa (40 percent) and was above average in the last five years (during which time financial markets became a strategic sector for IFC) (see Appendix B).

Project development results were weaker in the general manufacturing and services, funds, and health and education sectors. Figure 2.3 also shows that performance in IFC-supported projects in the general manufacturing and services sector (51 percent), and funds sector (46 percent) is below the all-sector average of 59 percent. Reflecting the fact that health and education are relatively new sectors for IFC investments, social sector projects that have been evaluated (13 to date) show below-average performance. Different levels of risk are a factor contributing to lower success rates. Investments

in funds tend to carry greater risks than investments in other sectors, while the relatively few evaluated investments in the social sectors have tended to face substantial structuring and market risks (for example, in developing commercially viable business models that are acceptable to the public in the country in which the investments are being made, given that the government remains the lead provider of these services in many countries).

C. Quality of the Sponsor

A low-quality sponsor can jeopardize the success of a project. Lower-quality sponsors—defined in terms of experience, financial capacity, commitment, and reputation—are associated with much lower development ratings (see table 2.2). Low sponsor quality was prevalent in about 40 percent of IFC commitments between 2002 and 2005, but sponsor quality can vary considerably by sector, and even within the same sector. For example, IFC investments in information and com-

---

Box 2.1. Examples of IFC Transport Investments in Brazil

In the early 1990s, Brazil's ports were suffering from low productivity, high operating costs, and inadequate maintenance. Handling charges in Brazil were roughly double those of international ports, and these high charges and inefficiencies were estimated to cost Brazilian exporters up to $5 billion per year in lost export opportunities. As part of its program to increase the competitiveness of the Brazilian economy, the government of Brazil passed a ports modernization law in 1993, which transferred port administration to state port authorities and required that the private sector operate the ports. IFC assisted in this privatization process by providing funding to the new private operators for upgrading and expanding port facilities.

- IFC supported the rehabilitation and expansion of the container terminal at the Port of Rio Grande, following the awarding of a 25-year lease in 1997 to a private consortium. IFC helped the company purchase four cranes, expand the length of the quay, and repair and upgrade existing facilities. The $50 million project has enhanced transport logistics in southern Brazil, resulting in increased exports and higher local employment, with more skilled and better-paid jobs.[4]
- The Port of Salvador in the Bahia state, in northeastern Brazil, was privatized in 2000 with the awarding of a 25-year lease to a private company. IFC arranged funding for part of a $20 million project to purchase two portainers (container cranes) and container-handling equipment, to pave the container storage

area, and to construct a warehouse and administration buildings. The private operator played an important role in increasing overall container volumes by nearly 300 percent between 2000 and 2005. As a successful project in a relatively poor and less developed part of Brazil, it played a vital role in increasing exports from the region, attracting other firms into the area (including companies such as Continental, Bridgestone, Pirelli, Monsanto, and Ford), and inducing follow-on investments in local transportation logistics.

- The government-built (and previously unused) container and steel-products terminal of Sepetiba is being operated under a 25-year lease awarded by the Port Authority of Rio de Janeiro in 1998. IFC is assisting the new private operator in a phased $140-million redevelopment of the container terminal, including the purchase of seven cranes, conversion of an existing dolphin berth into a straight quay, and construction of a rail connection. Largely owing to an intense competitive reaction from the neighboring port of Rio, Sepetiba's operations, in terms of container moves and profitability, have not yet met expectations. The project has, however, helped reduce congestion at ports across southeast Brazil, and the increased competition has resulted in a dramatic drop in tariffs for importers and exporters.

IEG's recent evaluation brief of IFC investments in the transport sector provides more detailed analysis of IFC's performance in this sector.[5]

Table 2.2. IFC Project Development Results Improve Significantly with the Presence of a High-Quality Sponsor

▶ When sponsor quality is high, projects are around 25 percentage points more likely to achieve high development ratings.

Sponsor quality	Percentage of projects with high development ratings	Percentage of projects with high investment ratings	Percentage of projects with high investment ratings—equity	Percentage of projects with high investment ratings—loans
High-quality sponsor	67	63	33	77
Low-quality sponsor	42	37	23	50
All projects	57	53	28	68

Source: IEG.

Note: Based on the risk profiling of 388 IFC investment operations that were approved during 1995–2000 and evaluated during 2000–05.

Table 2.3. **Product Market Risk Has a Strong Influence on IFC Project Development Results**

▶ Where a project's product market risk is high, projects are around 25 percentage points less likely to achieve high development ratings.

Product market risk	Percentage of projects with high development ratings	Percentage of projects with high investment ratings	Percentage of projects with high investment ratings—equity	Percentage of projects with high investment ratings—loans
Low product market risk	73	70	49	77
High product market risk	49	44	21	62
All projects	57	53	28	68

Source: IEG.

Note: Based on the risk profiling of 388 IFC investment operations that were approved during 1995–2000 and evaluated during 2000–05.

munications technology (soft infrastructure) are more often promoted by sponsors that are less well known and undercapitalized, and thus are riskier, than those involved in IFC transport operations (hard infrastructure).

D. Level of Product Market, Client Company, and Project Type Risks

IFC has had difficulties with assumptions about future product market changes, with a tendency to overestimate a company's growth prospects. Where a project's product market risk was high, projects were about 25 percentage points less likely to achieve high development ratings than when product market risk was low (table 2.3). The presence of high product market risk in newer commitments (those approved during 2002–05) is almost the same as in older commitments (those approved during 1995–2000), with around 60 percent of newly committed projects exhibiting high product market risk. IFC will need to manage this risk very carefully going forward.

Client company and project type risks can also affect the development performance. IFC has achieved better development results in carrying out follow-on or ancillary projects with known clients (67 percent) than with new clients (56 percent). This likely reflects the fact that with repeat clients an investor such as IFC can build up a long-term partnership with the company and help make it more economically and environmentally sus-

tainable. Similarly (but by project rather than client type), development results are generally better for expansion projects than for greenfield projects, with engineering and other risks generally more predictable for the former than the latter.

E. IFC Work Quality

IFC work quality, especially at approval, has been the most important success driver. Project development impact quality has been highly dependent on IFC work quality. When IFC work quality was rated high (satisfactory or excellent, see box 2.2 for a discussion of work quality metrics), IFC-supported projects achieved high development ratings 80 percent of the time. Conversely, where work quality was low (less than satisfactory), IFC-supported projects achieved high development impact quality only 20 percent of the time. High work quality can help mitigate other risk factors, such as business climate risk— as evidenced by the achievement of good results in Africa through good project execution, despite the generally unfavorable business climates (although work quality in Africa has generally lagged what has been achieved in other regions, see box 2.3).[6] As discussed in chapter 1, the decision that IFC takes at project entry, in terms of selecting viable projects and structuring them appropriately to mitigate risk, sets the tone for a new investment in terms of its likely development results. This is confirmed by project evaluations, which show that where appraisal and structuring work qual-

---

Box 2.2. IEG Evaluates IFC Work Quality across Three Underlying Indicators

IFC's overall work quality is rated on a four-point scale (excellent, satisfactory, partly unsatisfactory, and unsatisfactory) across the following three indicators:

- **Screening, appraisal, and structuring (at approval).** The extent to which IFC followed good practice standards, such as those identified in IFC credit notes. For example, with hindsight, did IFC identify key risk factors, mitigate them as much as possible, and arrive at realistic expectations for project and company performance? Actual results are compared with expectations and the main reasons for variance are analyzed, to assess whether IFC's assumptions were well-grounded in good practices, due diligence, and structuring, and the extent to which differences in actual results were due to extraneous effects, such as recognized but uncontrollable risks.
- **Supervision and administration (after approval).** Following approval and commitment, and through to eventual closure, this indicator assesses how well IFC carried out its supervision of an investment. For example, whether IFC was able to detect emerging problems in a company and respond expeditiously with appropriate and effective interventions.

- **Role and contribution (additionality).** Aligned with IFC's Article 1 guiding principles, this indicator describes the extent to which IFC played a catalytic role in an investment, and made a special contribution. For example, did IFC adhere to its corporate, country, and sector strategies and business principle, and was IFC timely and efficient in its dealings with the client?

As much as possible, IFC's work quality is evaluated independently of the project's outcome, to avoid bias in the ratings. For example, 12 percent of projects with high development ratings were nevertheless judged to have had low overall IFC work quality; and 32 percent of projects with low development ratings were still rated high for overall IFC work quality. Occasionally, however, actual project results can influence work quality ratings. Projects performing poorly can expose or exaggerate the weaknesses in IFC's structuring or supervision, which in the absence of significantly negative project performance might have gone undetected. Conversely, a project that is performing very well may be doing so despite shortfalls in IFC's work quality, which might, under different circumstances, have been more critical for outcome quality.

---

ity was high, IFC-supported projects achieved a 76 percent development success rate. Conversely, where appraisal and structuring work quality was low, IFC-supported projects achieved only a 21 percent development success rate.

Supervision quality is important, and improving, but insufficient to make up for low work quality at approval. Effective supervision also has a positive influence on development performance, with 73 percent of projects achieving high development ratings when supervision quality was high. This success rate fell to 32 percent when supervision quality was low. IFC supervision quality is currently the highest it has been since the current evaluation system was introduced in 1996 (85 percent satisfactory). This suggests that various quality enhancement steps taken by IFC between 1998 and 2001, while associated with a fall in quality as they were being introduced (which may reflect in part the need to meet more rigorous criteria from 1998), have started to have a positive effect (see figure 2.4). However, where

work quality at approval was low, high supervision work quality was not always able to compensate for shortfalls in due diligence or structuring at the front end, with 42-percent high development ratings in this situation, compared with 88 percent when both appraisal and supervision quality were high. These combinations of front-end and supervision work quality have a similar impact on investment success rates (see table 2.4). Most individual project evaluation lessons relate to work quality at approval, further stressing its significance to project development performance.[7]

Good supervision is nevertheless critical in ensuring strong client commitment to sound environmental and social practices. A forthcoming evaluation covering IFC's support for environmentally sustainable enterprises in Brazil, China, the Arab Republic of Egypt, Ghana, India, Kenya, Russian Federation, and Uganda[8] shows

The most important driver of project development performance has been IFC work quality.

Box 2.3. IFC Faced Considerable Challenges Pursuing Sustainable PSD in Africa

IFC is embarking on a bold growth plan in Africa, where it is seeking to double its investments by 2009

Between 1990 and 2006, IFC committed to 696 projects in Africa, with a total value of $4.6 billion. This represents 10 percent of IFC total commitments during this period, almost twice Africa's share of developing world GDP (5.6 percent). During the same period, Africa received just over $230 million (approximately 29 percent) of IFC's advisory services funding. Going forward, IFC is seeking to more than double its investments to about $900 million per year by 2009.

Ten years of evaluation show that IFC has faced major challenges doing business in Africa

While it is too early to evaluate the development results, investment success, and work quality of IFC's projects deriving from its 2007 Africa Strategy and the 2005 Bank Group Africa Action Plan,[9] reviewing 10 years of evaluation history of IFC's involvement in Africa highlights the challenges of doing business in the region. The development performance of IFC investment projects in Africa was below average (49 percent, compared with 61 percent for other regions between 1996 and 2006). Similarly, past results for IFC advisory services programs—the African Management Services Company and the African Project Development Facility—have not been particularly strong (although these programs were recently revamped).[10] Low development ratings in IFC investment projects reflected the lower quantifiable economic benefits of projects in Africa. IEG-IFC estimated that projects with at least satisfactory development results generated net quantifiable economic benefits of $1.50 for every $1 invested; whereas the yield from unsuccessful projects was just $0.10 for every $1 invested.[11]

IFC's experience also shows that smaller projects (below $5 million) in Africa performed less well (41 percent success rate, compared with 56 percent for larger operations) and that the quality of work (37 percent) was below average compared with larger projects (56 percent). The evaluation of IFC's experience also shows that financial market projects performed poorly and that financial market and general manufacturing projects were associated with weaker environmental and social effects than other projects, with lower compliance among IFC's clients. Two types of instruments did not work well: direct investments in SMEs and direct technical assistance to SMEs. This is important in the context of the relatively large presence of SMEs in the region, many of them operating in the informal sector, and given the priority role they play in IFC's Africa Strategy and the Africa Action Plan.

Scaling up successfully will require better project execution quality and concerted efforts to improve African business climates

The main reasons for the weak performance of private sector projects were a challenging business climate, a high operating-cost environment (administrative costs in Africa were twice those in other regions),[12] the relatively weak quality of IFC's work (45 percent of operations in Africa had high work quality, compared with 68 percent for operations in other regions), and IFC's willingness to take greater risks in its projects there,[13] as compared with other regions. Where the business climate and quality improved, so did IFC's results. For the success of its current strong scale up of operations in Africa, IFC will need to follow through on its efforts to improve quality control, including design, appraisal, and supervision throughout the project cycle, especially on smaller projects, and continue its focus on enhancing business climates in the region. Efforts to strengthen IFC–World Bank cooperation and to actively promote donor partnerships on initiatives for improving the business environment are, therefore, fundamental for private sector development and for better development impact of IFC's operations in Africa.

There have been several recent IFC strategic initiatives to significantly scale up and improve investment levels in Africa, in parallel with its high increase in commitments. These initiatives include the reorganization of advisory services into the Private Enterprise Partnership for Africa program, with a strong focus on business climate, financial market development, public-private partnerships in infrastructure and SMEs, as well as the strengthening of IFC's capabilities on the ground through stronger decentralization, all of which are a response to the above evaluation results.

---

that the most important success factor in delivering high environmental and social effects ratings (achieved in 67 percent of IFC operations overall) is a client's commitment to good environmental and social management. If the client is committed, with IFC's help it can build environmental management capacity and resources to identify and mitigate the environmental and social risks in a project, and proactively engage with project stakeholders and communities.[14] IEG evaluations find that where clients are developing sound environmental management systems, with close supervision by IFC, projects are more likely to deliver sustainable environmental and social performance.[15]

Figure 2.4. Supervision Quality Has Improved since 2001, Reflecting Several Quality Enhancement Steps

▶ IFC took a number of quality enhancement steps between 1998 and 2001. The impact of these steps is showing up in better supervision ratings since 2001. Assessing the impact of these steps on appraisal quality is more difficult because of the 5-year lag between appraisal and evaluation (meaning appraisal quality has not yet been evaluated ex post for those operations appraised since 2001). This issue does not arise in the case of supervision quality, which is already evident at the time of evaluation (that is, up to and including 2006).

That said, improved risk management at approval (which IEG assesses ex ante) suggests that these quality enhancements steps should have a positive impact on evaluated appraisal ratings in the coming years.

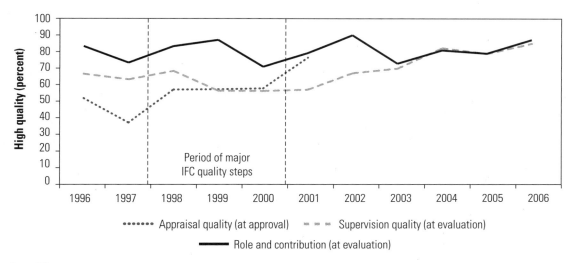

Source: IEG.

Table 2.4. Good Quality Supervision Cannot Compensate Fully for Weak Appraisal Quality

▶ Based on 627 operations evaluated between 1996 and 2006, appraisal and supervision quality have been key determinants of development success rates. High appraisal quality adds approximately 45–46 percentage points to IFC's development success rates while high supervision quality adds approximately 23–24 percentage points. The pattern is similar, though to a slightly lesser degree, for IFC investment success rates. Accordingly, high supervision quality cannot compensate fully for weak appraisal quality.

Work quality rating	Percentage of projects with high development ratings	Percentage of projects with high investment ratings
High appraisal quality, high supervision quality	88	77
High appraisal quality, low supervision quality	64	59
Low appraisal quality, high supervision quality	42	44
Low appraisal quality, low supervision quality	19	26

Source: IEG-IFC.

IFC's environmental and social effects work quality at appraisal is good but FI supervision is insufficient. Based on evaluations of environmental and social effects work quality since 2004, IFC's environmental appraisal for both FI and non–FI projects is good, but supervision quality of the FI portfolio is much lower compared with real-sector projects. New annual monitoring report templates, adopted in 2003, for various real-sector industries improved reporting quality and allowed IEG to better track the project compliance with at-appraisal objectives. IFC achieved high environmental and social effects appraisal ratings in 100 percent of the FI operations that were evaluated in 2005 and 2006, mainly because IFC's generic requirements for FI projects are quite straightforward and have been diligently translated into legal documents and commitment letters. There has, however, been a downward trend in the success rate of FI-project supervision work quality between 2004 and 2006, with only 47 percent of operations achieving high environmental and social effects supervision ratings in 2006. IFC has allocated most supervision resources to A-category and high-risk B-category projects.[16] As a consequence, IFC has not visited some lower-risk B-category projects and most FI projects. Some FIs that IFC finances may have thousands of subprojects—if even only a small percentage is screened to the B–category, incorporating environmental and social effects risks, the cumulative impact of many subprojects could be significant. There is thus a serious gap in IFC's knowledge of project environmental and social effects in FI operations, and in environmental and social effects ratings themselves, a fourth of which IEG has been unable to validate, given the lack of information or litigation/legal barriers to obtaining information. In response to observed gaps in environmental and social effects supervision, IFC is taking a number of steps to improve its performance, including visiting FI projects with a high-risk profile or with deficiencies in their environmental management systems every three years. Environmental and social management system deficiencies may be addressed without a site visit. Time will tell whether these steps are successful.[17]

Type of Financing Has Implications for Development Performance

Foreign currency financing can be problematic, especially for nonexporting SMEs. A common theme highlighted by IEG evaluations in last 10 years is the lack of term local-currency financing, especially in Africa, and the substantial investment constraints placed on firms with a high dependence on domestic currency revenues,

particularly if exposed to exchange rate devaluation.[18] This is because of the mismatch between income (in local currency) and expenditure commitments (in foreign currency). An extreme example is that of the Argentinean banks that borrowed heavily in dollars in the 1990s, and following a one-time, drastic, 70-percent devaluation of the Argentinean peso in 2001, were left with large deficits in their balance sheets. Other examples include devaluations in Turkey and Brazil in the 1990s, which had particularly adverse impacts on second-tier companies in which IFC invested.[19]

IFC is seeking to address the need for more local currency financing, with increased loans and guarantees in local currency. As figure 2.5 shows, IFC has substantially increased its local-currency-denominated financial products in recent years. IFC is able to offer medium- to long-term loans and hedges in 28 emerging market currencies. IFC's largest recipient of local currency loans has been Mexico, followed by India and China (by amount), although IFC has now provided local currency operations to 16 African countries (the CFA franc zone, which includes Benin, Burkina Faso, Cameroon, Chad, Côte d'Ivoire, Mali, Senegal, Togo, plus, the Gambia, Ghana, Guinea, Kenya, Madagascar, Nigeria, Swaziland, and South Africa). IFC has also facilitated a number of local-currency bond issues, including in Brazil and Morocco. IFC nonetheless recognizes it could provide more local currency products, given the high demand for them. IFC is exploring ways to provide local currency financing in markets where there are no hedging alternatives available, through the crea-tion of a global fund that provides local currency hedges for loans disbursed by IFC.[20] IFC is also carrying out preparatory work for a CFA franc, domestic-currency bond issue, which will allow IFC to establish its credit in the market so it can support local financial institutions by offering structured products to finance the private sector throughout the region.

In reaching SMEs generally, direct engagement has not proven to be very successful for IFC. An internal IEG evaluation in 2000 found that direct lending to SMEs was nei-

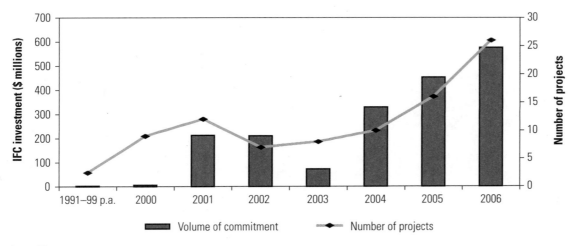

Figure 2.5. IFC Is Increasing Its Provision of Local Currency Financing

▶ Prior to 2001, IFC made one or two low-value loans each year in local currency, each typically under the value of $10 million-equivalent. Since 2004, IFC has increased its local currency lending, averaging nearly $25 million-equivalent per investment, and has also started to provide a broadly similar number of local currency guarantees.

Source: IFC.

Note: Figures do not include local currency options offered to, but not yet accepted by, IFC clients or some commitments that have yet to be disbursed.

ther an effective nor an efficient model for IFC. The evaluation found that IFC faced unacceptably high administrative costs lending directly to SMEs, and should focus more on FIs as a vehicle to reach SMEs. IFC subsequently shifted its SME approach to a wholesale model through FIs, an approach for which a 2007 evaluation provides continued support.[21] IFC has also moved to a more wholesale approach on the advisory services side of its business (under the Private Enterprise Partnership), by working with groups of SMEs as part of a single project.

Nature of Linkages between Investment and Advisory Services Activities Is Also Important
Two forthcoming evaluations highlight the potential benefits of linkages between investment and advisory services activities. IEG-IFC will soon report in detail on the performance of the Private Enterprise Partnership advisory services program in Eastern Europe and Central Asia,[22] as well as on IFC's results in financing micro, small, and medium enterprises through financial intermediaries.[23] One finding

that emerges from both evaluations is the potential development gains for clients through IFC's synergies between its investment and advisory services activities. In the Private Enterprise Partnership, for example, sectorwide initiatives integrating advisory services with IFC investments achieved higher development results than individual transaction-based links. On the other hand, advisory strategy and projects were largely developed and delivered independently of IFC investment staff expertise, diminishing potential synergies and results. In helping microfinance intermediaries, meanwhile, IFC has achieved successful results where it has provided, along with other multilateral development bank shareholders, technical assistance grant funds to cover costs involved with, for instance, establishment and training alongside equity investments.

Evaluation Provides a Basis for Better IFC Results
Evaluation has helped promote a development effectiveness culture within IFC. Building on IFC Management's initiative, in 1996,

IFC and IEG copioneered a monitoring and self-evaluation system for IFC's investment operations. More recently, IFC constructed a monitoring and self-evaluation system for its advisory services operations, developed broadbased performance scorecards, and introduced real-time development results tracking the project life cycle for the whole portfolio.[24] These steps are aligned with evaluation report recommendations made since the late 1990s for IFC to identify and monitor development results from the point of project approval onward and to establish an incentive structure that emphasizes development-based effectiveness.

Evaluation has revealed some key drivers of development results and areas for process improvement and strategy. As presented throughout this chapter, a decade of evaluation has identified several factors that have had a significant determinant effect on project-level development results. The knowledge of these drivers influences IFC decision making about issues, such as engagement in countries with high business climate risk and which sectors to emphasize or de-emphasize. Evaluation findings on IFC appraisal and supervision performance, beginning with IEG's first annual review (covering operations evaluated in 1996), also helped inform some of the steps that IFC Management took in the late 1990s, such as setting up a Credit Department, portfolio units, and an equity desk, as well as developing tighter environmental and social appraisal and supervision procedures. Finally, country and sector evaluations have fed into the Bank Group's country and sector strategies.

Management has adopted the vast majority of IEG recommendations. Table 2.5 sets out key evaluation recommendations, findings, and impacts in the areas mentioned above. IFC Management and IEG, together, track IFC's progress in implementing recommendations from evaluation reports in a Management Action Tracking Record. An internal report found that, as of early 2006, about three-quarters of IEG recommendations were rated as having a "high" or "substantial" level of adoption by IFC Management.

Table 2.5. Evaluation Findings Have Provided a Basis for Better IFC Results in Three Main Areas

Year	1. Promoting a development effectiveness culture	2. Identifying key development success drivers	3. Laying the foundations for better IFC appraisal
1996	IEG (with IFC management) copioneers new evaluation system for investment operations		
1997		IEG finding: More realistic market assessments (less optimism bias) would improve results	Recommendation: Ensure projections take full account of identified risks
1998	IEG recommendation: establish development effectiveness objectives at approval	Finding: Large investments tend to perform better	Recommendations: Set up independent appraisal and/or credit committee to improve due diligence; adopt Project Supervision Records; carry out more supervision from field offices
1999	Recommendation: Introduce development-based incentives	Finding: IFC performs best in high risk countries	
2000	Recommendation: Describe expected development results at appraisal, and monitor during supervision	Finding: Lack of local currency funding a major problem for IFC clients	Recommendation: Improve FI monitoring of environmental effects of subprojects
2001		Recommendation: Consider wholesale approach to SMEs through FIs rather than direct lending	
2002		Finding: Better results where business climates improved	
2003	Recommendation: Establish self-evaluation systems for noninvestment operations	Finding: Good IFC work quality especially key where business climate risk is high	
2004		Finding: Four key results drivers explain some two thirds of IFC results	Recommendation: Involve portfolio managers early on in the appraisal process
2005	IEG inputs into new evaluation system for advisory services operations	Finding: IFC performs well in countries with improving business climates	Recommendation: Track IFC's role and contribution through the supervision stage
2006		Finding: Local currency finance key for nonexporting SMEs	Recommendation: Ensure effective mainstreaming of environmental appraisal and supervision
Overall impact	Better measurement of, and incentives for, development impact	Influences IFC decision making, including how to target and tailor operations in high-risk countries	Strengthened procedures and structures for appraisal and supervision
Example of impact	Real-time Development Outcome Tracking System and Long-Term Performance Awards (linked to achieved development impact) since 2005	IFC is increasing the availability of local currency financing	IFC established a credit department in 1998

Note: All findings and recommendations cited above are contained in IEG-IFC evaluations.

Strategic Implications for IFC

Evaluation findings have shown that IFC has generally made sound corporatewide strategic choices over the past decade. IFC has extended its reach in frontier markets and has achieved above-average development results, overall, in its strategic countries and sectors—particularly through its infrastructure operations.

Nonetheless, performance can always be improved and IFC is rightly looking for ways to strengthen its development contribution. IFC is seeking to increase its development impact by growing its business rapidly and decentralizing its operations. As it pursues a higher level of activity under a new organizational structure, IFC must develop more country-focused planning, adopt new incentives and mechanisms for IFC–World Bank cooperation in areas of synergy (such as business climate development), and pay extra close attention to work quality issues. It is also crucial that IFC incorporate in its strategic vision the possible growth and institutional implications of the next major correction in the international markets.

IFC Is Pursuing an Ambitious Growth Plan While Further Decentralizing

Since 1998, IFC has broadly pursued five strategic priorities, generally with above-average development performance. IFC's 1998 strategy (the first major strategic review since 1991) provided the initial market and sector grounding for the five strategic priorities that

IFC has pursued in recent years: (i) greater focus on frontier markets; (ii) build long-term partnerships with emerging global players in developing countries; (iii) differentiate through sustainability; (iv) address constraints to private sector growth in infrastructure, health, and education; and (v) develop local financial markets. Evaluation results from the past decade broadly support these priorities, with IFC generally achieving better development and investment results in the projects it has supported in its strategic countries and sectors (with the exception of the social sectors), as well as with larger, repeat clients.

Overall, IFC has achieved above-average development performance in strategic countries and sectors.

In 2005, IFC embarked on an ambitious new growth plan. IFC's 1998 strategy also envisaged a potential doubling of IFC approvals by 2005 (from about $3 billion per year, to about $6 billion per year).[1] This goal was broadly achieved. In light of better development performance in most of its areas of strategic focus, IFC's 2005 strategy called for IFC to accelerate the implementation of its strategic priorities, as a means to maximize its development impact and optimize the use of its capital base. In this context, the strategy called for an increase in investment operations by approximately 35 percent overall, and by nearly 100 percent in frontier countries by 2008.

This growth plan was supplemented in 2006 with six high-priority goals, and a challenge to further decentralize operations. The 2006 strategy extended the growth plan until 2009, and set out six high-priority goals to be achieved during the 2006–09 period. These goals are: (i) greater development impact, (ii) improved World Bank Group cooperation, (iii) leadership in standard setting, (iv) improved client satisfaction, (v) sound finances, and (vi) strong staff. The revised strategy also laid out the challenges to IFC of further decentralizing its operations, bolstering its human resources (for example, building and developing diverse talent, enhancing corporate and staff incentives, and accelerating decentralization), developing sufficient risk management and financial capacity, and ensuring effective management of its advisory services. There has been a conscious trend toward the decentralization of IFC operations in the last 10 years, with the number of IFC investment officers in the field more than doubled during that time.[2] The latest decentralization initiative, confirmed by IFC Management in early 2007, is bolder than previous ones, however, in that it proposes the same level of relative growth in field-based investment staff in just three years, by 2010.

The latest decentralization initiative is bolder than previous ones.

For analytical purposes, IFC's strategic objectives can be seen to cover four perspectives of a strategy-focused organization.[3] IFC's strategy would map onto these perspectives as follows:

- *Stakeholder and client perspective.* To meet the expectations of its stakeholders, in strengthening its development impact, IFC is proposing to scale up its activities in all of its focus sectors and regions, especially in frontier countries and regions, and to expand its investments in infrastructure, health, and education, as well as strengthen the development of local financial markets. Meanwhile, IFC is offering a value proposition to its clients, based on pursuing differentiation through sustainability, promoting "South-South" investment partnerships, supplying a range of complementary technical assistance and investment instruments, and improving client relations and satisfaction.

- *Internal process perspective.* To meet these objectives toward its stakeholders and clients, IFC is internally undertaking major initiatives for decentralization, strengthening World Bank cooperation, improving client relations processes, and reducing processing time.[4]

- *Human capital perspective.* The above strategic objectives have led to the pursuit of further redeployment of staff that would allow the creation of a global/local institution. This has created demands for careful institutional knowledge management based on local business originators and portfolio managers, and global specialists that will transfer international development knowledge.

- *Financial and measurement perspective.* Finally, IFC strategy is underpinned by the pursuit of stronger risk-management capacity to support growth, sound finances, and a technological platform that can facilitate internal processes to help IFC be more effective with its clients.

Going forward, there are opportunities for improvement for IFC across each perspective.

Stakeholder and Client Perspective: IFC Needs to Adopt a Deeper Country Focus and Emphasize Distributional Issues

Prioritizing high-need countries remains a highly relevant approach for IFC. IFC has achieved high development ratings through its pursuit of a frontier strategy, catalyzing investment in high-risk and low-income countries (including a number that have been affected by conflict) and sectors. The subsequent graduation of many frontier countries into environments more conducive to private sector investment is the driving force behind these positive results, and

Figure 3.1. Many Nonfrontier Countries Are as Lacking in Banking Capacity as Frontier Countries

▶ In terms of banking capacity (proxied by the proportion of private-sector domestic credit to GDP), there is close similarity between frontier and nonfrontier countries. Excluding China, which accounts for approximately 23 percent of developing country GDP, the average banking capacity of nonfrontier MICs has stagnated in the last 10 years at about 40 percent. Average banking capacity in frontier countries has, however, grown to the point where there is little to distinguish the banking depth of frontier from nonfrontier countries.

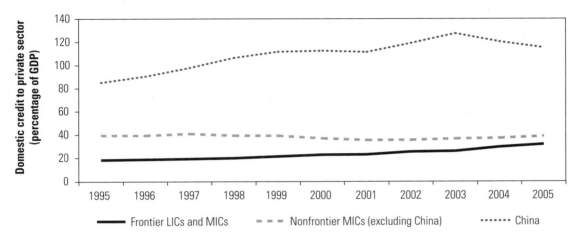

Source: World Bank Group, Global Development Finance database.

thus highlights the importance of Bank and IFC efforts to improve business climate quality. This is of utmost importance in Africa, which has fallen far behind other developing markets in terms of investment risk and private investment.

Major private sector development needs are not, however, found exclusively in frontier countries. Many nonfrontier MICs, the mainstay of the developing world, also have substantial PSD needs. The binary split of the world into frontier/nonfrontier has its shortcomings. First, many countries have migrated from the former to the latter category (such that frontier markets account for a much smaller share of developing country GDP than they did in 1997). Second, many countries that are currently classified as nonfrontier have similar enabling infrastructure needs as do frontier countries. Moreover, there are significant constraints to doing business in nonfrontier MICs, relative to high-income countries, including financial markets and infrastructure development that hinder the competitiveness of firms in these countries (which account for about 85 percent of developing country GDP and where approximately

one-third of all people who live on less than $2 per day reside):

- The banking capacity of nonfrontier countries is generally no deeper than frontier country banking capacity (see figure 3.1), and is much lower than in high-income countries.[5] Financial markets are particularly underdeveloped in Latin American MICs.[6] Lack of banking capacity keeps the cost of doing business high for many countries, especially where term local-currency financing has been lacking and limits poverty-reducing growth.[7]

- Infrastructure shortages are notable in many nonfrontier MICs. The Private Provision of Infrastructure average for these countries, at 1.6 percent of GDP, is higher than the average 0.9 percent of GDP for frontier countries.[8] However, the cost of trading across borders nonetheless remains high, keeping the cost of doing business higher than it might be otherwise.[9] Infrastructure shortcomings of this kind are particularly important for many MICs, such as Egypt, Mexico, and the Philippines, which are

There are significant constraints to doing business in middle-income countries.

heavily dependent on otherwise low-cost industrial exports.[10]

- High informality that reduces the productivity of the law-abiding, otherwise efficient companies.[11]
- There are sizable low-income and/or high-risk regions within nonfrontier MICs, which reflects the unequal development of the private sector and economic growth in these countries. IFC is starting to measure its commitments in the frontier regions of 20 MICs, but does not yet know to what extent it is reaching low-income and/or high-risk regions across all MICs.

When private capital flows have been more abundant, IFC has made less of a unique, pioneering contribution in MICs—emphasizing the need for IFC to carefully consider country dynamics in defining its additionality. When private capital flows were relatively high in the mid-1990s, the institution was less successful in providing a unique role and contribution. IFC also achieved noticeably worse development and investment ratings in MICs when its role and contribution were rated as less than satisfactory. When role and contribution was rated low, only 6 percent of IFC-supported projects achieved high development ratings, generally, compared with 71 percent when IFC's role and contribution was rated high—a bigger differential than for IFC operations in low-income countries.[12]

The need for a deeper country approach is amplified when looking at IFC's below-average results in countries with low banking capacity. While IFC prioritizes investments in the financial sector (together with infrastructure and social sector investments) and is, on the whole, reaching countries with below-average banking capacity (where the share of private sector credit to GDP has been less than the developing country average of 35 percent), its results in these countries are much weaker than in countries with above-average banking capacity (where the

Where IFC's role and contribution was low in MICs, only 6 percent of projects achieved high development ratings.

share of private sector credit to GDP has been greater than 35 percent). Sixty-seven percent of IFC financial sector commitments between 1996 and 2006 were in countries with low banking sector depth, while 25 percent of IFC financial sector commitments were in countries with high banking sector depth.[13] However, the development results of IFC-supported financial sector projects in countries where banking sector depth was low—which includes 39 countries in Africa—were lower than those in countries with high banking capacity. Only 55 percent of IFC-supported financial sector projects were rated highly in low banking capacity countries, compared with 71 percent in countries with above-average banking capacity (see table 3.1). These results highlight the need for IFC to work closely with governments and other development partners to optimize IFC's additionality and the development potential of these investments, for example, in financial intermediaries providing support to micro, small, and medium enterprises (which a forthcoming evaluation confirms is an effective way for IFC to reach them).[14] IFC also has a role to play in identifying and facilitating regulatory changes that reduce corruption and/or the pursuit of anticompetitive practices (which have been a problem in low banking capacity countries such as Senegal and Malawi).[15]

A forthcoming evaluation of the Private Enterprise Partnership also shows that greater country tailoring is needed in some of IFC's advisory services operations. In its Private Enterprise Partnership program, a forthcoming evaluation shows that IFC has tended to replicate product line initiatives rather than tailor them to individual country needs. Moreover, senior staff took brief needs-assessment trips to ascertain the appropriateness of new projects, but these assessments were not thorough enough to prepare or sufficiently adapt many projects adequately to country-specific needs and conditions before project launch.[16]

IFC could strengthen its commitment to country needs through the use of systematic indicators for PSD progress. Clearly identi-

Table 3.1. IFC's Financial Sector Development Success Rates Are Lower Where Banking Capacity Is Weak

Level of banking capacity	Number of projects	Percentage of projects with high development ratings	Percentage of projects with high investment ratings
Above-average (private sector credit share > 35%)	38	71	76
Below-average (private sector credit share < 35%)	121	55	58
Total	159	59	62

Source: IEG; and World Bank Group, Global Development Finance database.

Note: Projects were evaluated between 2001 and 2006.

fying individual country needs is challenging and the ability of IFC to respond to these needs will depend on IFC's own capacity in the country, particularly in relation to other sources of private finance. Nonetheless, together with the Bank and country governments, IFC could develop and pursue a set of PSD indicators that would help guide its strategy and operations in each country, bearing in mind its own capacity constraints. These indicators could include the level of private, gross, fixed-capital formation; banking sector depth; and other indicators of access to finance as well as private provision of infrastructure in a country. Some indicators along these lines were included for select countries in the 2005 World Bank Group Africa Action Plan.[17]

Tackling quality of growth and pure market distributional issues will be important, as will recognizing that poverty has a strong rural origin. Evaluation has shown that the quality of economic growth and the distribution of income matters in reducing the number of poor people.[18] Poverty continues to show a strong rural origin, and an explicit recognition of this in IFC's strategy would be appropriate. A focus on the agribusiness sector, where IFC operations have had beneficial impacts for farmers and producers through linkage programs, could be useful in this respect.[19] Rural microfinance is equally important,

though evaluation findings suggest that the cost basis of rural schemes may be higher than for urban-based microfinance institutions because of the greater geographical spread of clients.[20] Box 3.1 provides examples of successful agribusiness and rural microfinance operations. As IFC decentralizes further, one priority would be an environmental and social strategy at the country level to identify and develop high-impact projects with widespread demonstration effects. Such projects include those with meaningful and effective safeguards to offset environmental and social damages, projects aimed at capitalizing on the possibilities for developing countries to make money from environmental and social protection, and also those designed to facilitate greater involvement of women entrepreneurs. From IEG's ongoing study in the area of environmental performance, actions relating to the environment and climate change are emerging as a priority area.[21] Finally, given its growing and evident impact upon lower-income groups, in this same area of market distribution considerations, IFC might evaluate its role in the remittances market, either in the efforts that many are making to reduce the costs of transfers or in the provision of better financial services to the population involved in these flows.[22]

IFC will need to continue efforts to increase the provision of local currency financing. As

Box 3.1. Examples of Successful Agribusiness and Rural Finance Operations

An agribusiness operation in West Africa with substantial social impacts: The project was a palm oil operation in a west African country. Operations would include the planting of palm trees as well as establishing a mill to extract oil. The expansion was a follow-up investment following the privatization of a rubber plantation (the palm operation was a new project on the plantation). The client company inherited workers as well as the social services infrastructure (schools and health care) of the region. The project allowed for more productive use of the labor force and facilitated maintenance of the social infrastructure. The company also provided two smallholder programs with extension services around the industrial plantation. The outgrower scheme supported by the company provided linkages to surrounding planters and for local private businesses. The project brought improved living standards to the small outgrowers as they gained access to new plantation techniques and practices, with the outgrowers earning more revenues than they would have earned from subsistence farming, as well as gaining access to improved physical infrastructure.

An integrated approach to microfinance, including fee-based advisory services, with significant rural development impacts: The project was to support the expansion and development of one of the first private-sector microfinance institutions responding to the credit needs of the rural poor, a large market segment not properly served by the formal and informal financial system. IFC invested equity together with a pre- and post-investment advisory services program (the client microfinance institution realized that apart from microcredit, rural households have a significant need for advisory assistance to improve their microbusinesses). Subsequently, IFC reoriented its strategy to provide three services in an integrated manner:

(i)   *Financial services*—microcredit and microinsurance (for example, life, rainfall, crops);
(ii) *Agricultural/business development services*—advisory services on productivity enhancements (vaccinations, pest management) and alternate input/output market linkages; and
(iii) *Institutional development services*—advisory services on the formation of producers' groups for enhancing bargaining power and lowering transaction costs, capacity building, accounting, and information technology systems.

IFC is now engaged in providing credit as well as technical assistance and advisory services to rural small-enterprise owners, farmers, village self-help groups and other rural service providers. The revised strategy has been appreciated by its target customers, with the total client base increasing to almost 20,000 by the end of 2005. IFC has not only generated additional fee income, but also significant goodwill among its clients.

---

various evaluations have shown in the last 10 years, term local-currency financing is insufficient in many countries. Where term local-currency financing is unavailable and companies resort to hard-currency financing, they are often unable to match their assets (denominated in local currency) and liabilities (borrowings, typically denominated in foreign currency), thus making them especially vulnerable to exchange rate fluctuations. This has been a particular problem in Africa, where exchange rate volatility, combined with commodity price fluctuations in economies with limited diversity, has meant that foreign currency borrowing has proven costly for African firms.[23] While IFC has increased its local-currency financial products, the need for more local currency financing remains substantial.

Tackling quality of growth and distributional issues will be important.

Finding a workable model for social sector investments is also an area for improvement. Based on the 13 evaluations to date, IFC has had a weak record in its social sector investments. Nonetheless, it has achieved some successes, notably through innovative structuring (through Public Private Partnerships) and where the operations have targeted a market segment that is not significantly exposed to foreign exchange risk.[24] Since education and health care is typically paid for in local currency, some operations have failed due to currency devaluations that have made their foreign currency exposures (including IFC foreign-currency loans) an unsustainable burden. IFC is, encouragingly, increasing its use of innovative, nonconventional structuring, although public acceptance of the role of private provisioning in social services remains variable.

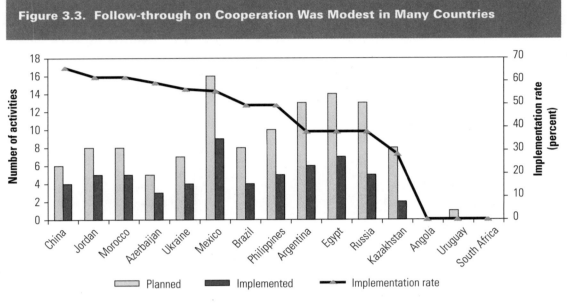

Figure 3.3. Follow-through on Cooperation Was Modest in Many Countries

Source: IEG.

anced out the factors that facilitate cooperation (see table 3.2).[29] Incentives to cooperate with the Bank and exploit synergies, within a better country-level operational framework, particularly to develop the enabling infrastructure for private sector development, are urgently needed. Efforts announced by IFC in March 2007 to create more structured processes to enable greater input into its advisory services operations by Bank staff are, in this respect, encouraging.[30]

Human Capital Perspective: Ensure Robust Work Quality as IFC Decentralizes

IFC's strategy predicts greater development impacts through a higher level of activities and better quality. However, this is difficult to achieve in the short run, as the experience in the late 1990s illustrates. Change is usually disruptive, and change in several dimensions at the same time can be especially disruptive. During a previous period of major organizational change, 1998–2001, IFC supervision quality—an important driver of development success rates—fell sharply. In these years, IFC carried out numerous quality enhancement steps, including the establishment of a Credit Department and portfolio desks, and introduced new environmental review procedures. Despite these measures (or because of them, since they raised standards in some cases for projects that had already been approved), supervision quality was high in only 56 percent of IFC investment operations in these years, compared with an average of 73 percent in other years. The quality enhancement steps have, overall, helped IFC to improve supervision quality, though with lagged implementation (supervision quality started improving from 2002).

IFC has improved risk management and supervision quality in South Asia as it has decentralized, but with more modest volume growth than in other regions. IFC has improved its risk management at approval in South Asia with decentralization of activities in the region, reducing sponsor risk and market risk (table 3.3), while also achieving above-average supervision quality.[31] This suggests that decentralization has improved quality at different stages of the project

The CAS holds less sway on IFC's deliverables than the World Bank's.

Table 3.2. Drivers and Inhibitors of World Bank–IFC Cooperation

Factor	Example as driver	Example as inhibitor
Institutional level		
High-level direction	Strong top-down messages encourage staff to seek out cooperative opportunities	
Organizational structure	Joint departments increase information sharing between staff with similar interests	Different reporting lines: IFC investment department and regional strategy units vs. Bank country office; modest IFC ownership for CAS deliverables
Cross-institutional recognition and incentives		Lack of recognition for contributions to work of the other institution
Country level		
Level of country manager interaction	Greater information exchange and strategic planning through joint management teams, regular, systematic information exchanges (e.g., through joint staff meetings)	Limited interaction constrains information sharing and/or breeds misperceptions
Country office setup	(i) Strong IFC country office staff presence (ii) Co-located offices	(i) Lack of IFC country office staff (ii) Offices in different cities or another part of the same city
Client govenment demand	Strong government push for cooperation	
Project level		
Project timeline	Similar timetables for completion	Incompatible timelines slow project
Perceived conflicts of interest		Reputational and commercial risks from inappropriate information flows
Individual level		
Personality, relationships, and perceptions	Some staff more likely to communicate across institutional boundaries; prior working relationships provide openings	(i) Perception that culture of other institution is too different to exploit synergies (ii) Staff too busy to seek out counterparts

Source: IEG.

cycle. However, this improvement has occurred with more modest volume growth than in other regions.[32] Employing more staff in the field and increased volumes of operations may go hand-in-hand (lack of local presence in the Ukraine in the 1990s was a key reason IFC was behind EBRD in realizing investment opportunities in the country)[33] but could take time. This suggests the need for a steady roll-out in the decentralization of IFC activities while pursuing a growth agenda, and care-

Table 3.3. With Decentralization, the South Asia Region Improved Its Risk Management in Key Areas

High-risk factor	South Asia: Change in operations exhibiting a high-risk factor between periods 1995–2000 and 2002–05 (percent)	Other regions: Change in operations exhibiting a high-risk factor between periods 1995–2000 and 2002–05 (percent)
Product market risk	−22	−6
Sponsor risk	−14	−3
Review intensity risk	−23	−3

Source: IEG.

ful monitoring and management of the inherent risks, so as to learn from experience and mitigate any volume/project-execution quality trade-offs.

The greatest risk in a decentralization process is the loss of global knowledge. Knowledge is one of the most important intangible assets that IFC uses to promote private sector development. As figure 3.4 illustrates, IFC faces a knowledge-retention challenge in that the majority of staff attending core credit training in 2001 and 2002 are no longer active with IFC (implying inefficient use of training resources by IFC as well as a knowledge drain). This sort of retention issue is amplified in an organization that, as previous evaluations have shown, does not have the best record in knowledge capture and sharing, and where knowledge often resides with

Figure 3.4. IFC Faces a Knowledge-Retention Challenge

▶ Since 2001, all new IFC investment officers are required to attend core credit training, as a means to ensure that IFC transaction quality is consistent and of a high quality.

An analysis of past attendees of this core credit training shows that more than a half of attendees who completed the course in either 2001 or 2002 are no longer working at IFC. While there are more new trainees now than in 2002 (192 in 2006 compared with 52 in 2002) this still presents a major knowledge-retention challenge for IFC, as it seeks to increase transaction work quality, unless IFC develops a better record of retaining staff that have completed the training more recently.

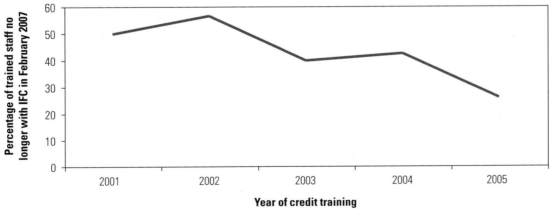

Source: IFC.

a few very experienced individuals rather than a unit or department.[34] Finally, given the decentralization process and redeployment of staff, IFC will need to ensure that it protects not only its brand but, more importantly, its organizational culture and global knowledge, guarding against the creation of numerous local cultures that adversely dilute IFC's "style" and impact.

IFC might learn from the experiences of the Bank in knowledge sharing within a more dispersed organization. The Bank has extensive experience in trying to ensure effective global/local knowledge synergies. The Bank's regions have developed internal knowledge-sharing tools and activities. However, as a 2003 evaluation showed,[35] in the absence of a mandate defining the regions' internal knowledge-sharing responsibilities, their scope has varied. And since 2000, the Bank's regions have increasingly focused on extending their knowledge-sharing activities to the transfer and brokering of knowledge with clients, but this has not been matched with enhanced attention to internal knowledge sharing. Moreover, while Bank operations are increasingly multisectoral in approach, the bulk of knowledge capture and sharing is organized by network and sector. In interviews conducted for a study by IEG-World Bank, staff noted that the "silo" structure of the internal knowledge-sharing function did not meet the needs of multisectoral operational work. Additionally, there was inadequate coordination between network knowledge-sharing activities and the country and project teams. Few network internal knowledge-sharing activities were embedded directly in core work processes.[36]

Leveling up the quality of IFC's environmental supervision of FI operations should be a central consideration. In addition to below-average supervision in the financial sector, discussed earlier, evaluation has also highlighted a low role and contribution of IFC in this sector. More often than not this was due to IFC not having delivered on its expected contribution—including helping these institutions develop adequate in-house environmental and social monitoring capability. In theory, greater on-the-ground presence should help IFC improve the supervision of the environmental and social effects of its operations, and provide a greater role and contribution, as it potentially enables IFC to work more closely with clients in promoting good environmental and social practices. To maximize this opportunity, IFC will need to make sure it continues mainstreaming environmental and social responsibilities throughout its investment staff and that the appropriate specialist capacity is provided to support effective supervision of the environmental and social effects of FI operations.

Effective local recruitment, especially in Africa, will also be important. Overall, IFC faces fierce competition from the market to attract high-quality investment officers. Recruitment challenges are particularly acute in Africa. Despite its increasing focus on development results, IFC's incentive regime is still geared toward the level of activities and speed of delivery of projects. Africa, where projects outside the extractive and infrastructure sectors are usually quite small and gestation periods are lengthy, has historically not been perceived as an attractive place to work. IFC has found it difficult to attract significant numbers of high-performing investment officers to commit to working in the region (although recent efforts to increase staffing in the regional office in Johannesburg appear to be gaining some traction).[37] Compensation is also a problem, particularly in light of overall shortages in the number of suitably qualified, locally based personnel.

Financial and Measurement Perspective: Prepare for the Next Major Market Correction and Improve Development Impact Measurement

While risk management and business climate risk has improved, this pattern could easily be reversed. IFC's development and investment success rates are heavily influenced by the quality of risk management of its projects, as well as the quality of the business climates in which they operate. IFC has improved its risk management at approval since 2001, to the extent that it been able to balance the increased risk associated

Box 3.3 Examples of IFC's Countercyclical Role during Previous Crises

Korea

Corporate restructuring: IFC helped foreign investors to take over a failing security firm. The investors restructured the firm, introduced new marketing methods, and issued new financial instruments (dollar-denominated corporate bonds). The result was a successful corporate turnaround, with retention of jobs and regained market share. Other investors subsequently copied this deal structure, and the company was ultimately bought by a domestic bank, as foreign investors exited.

Introduction of securitization: IFC helped in one of the first, cross-border, lease asset transactions in Korea in the wake of the Asian crisis. The transaction was expected to provide much needed liquidity and term funding to the client company, and to demonstrate the feasibility of securitization of domestic assets in the country. Although placement of the securitized notes in international markets was limited, the transaction had a capacity-building effect on local agencies, institutions, and counterparts, and showed that securitizing Korean assets could be done.

Russia

Corporate restructuring and liquidity: IFC invested in a restructuring fund after the Russian Crisis of 1998. The fund was to provide additional equity for corporate restructuring, capital investment, and working capital. The investment was successful because it provided valuable capital to the portfolio companies to help them weather the crisis when external capital was scarce. IFC's investment was catalytic in terms of enabling new capital injections and helped the fund managers to stay intact during hard years of fundraising.

Turkey:

Helping industrial clients through market turbulence: IFC played a similar countercyclical role in Turkey. IFC has supported its large industrial clients through several periods of market turbulence since the mid-1990s, and during the clients' emergence as major engines of economic growth within the country.[40]

with new investments in frontier markets with appropriate project and investment structuring. Pursuing a rapid-growth agenda while reorganizing IFC may have an impact on the quality of risk management, however, and IFC will need to carefully monitor this to avoid a decline in its success rates. Moreover, there is the growing threat of a significant global economic slowdown, including developing country economies, which would likely affect the development effectiveness of IFC's operations. (In addition, it could have an impact on IFC's profitability, which has depended heavily in recent years on returns of IFC's equity investments, and will depend in coming years on the ability to convert considerable unrealized gains into actual returns; see appendix B). An explicit recognition of the potential for a major correcting event, given a more complex global financial system, its possible impacts on the developing countries, and the risk-mitigating actions and products conceived by IFC to serve its clients, would strengthen IFC's strategic vision. In general, within this context, continued efforts to improve risk-management systems[38] and to prepare for the next major shift in the international markets, including perhaps the development of new risk-mitigating products, will need to be at the forefront of IFC's strategic planning.[39]

IFC is pursuing a rapid growth agenda while decentralizing.

IFC's role as a countercyclical lender will be more important than ever in the event of a global economic downturn. Box 3.3 outlines some examples of how IFC played a countercyclical role in the respective crises in the Republic of Korea, Russia, and Turkey. Learning from past experiences, IFC will need to look for similar opportunities for a value-added role in the event of a new economic downturn and a sudden cessation or withdrawal of private capital flows directed at developing countries.

Strengthening capacity for evaluation and its application will also be important. Increasingly in recent years, IFC's strategic directions have been informed by evaluation findings. This has been aided by the breadth and depth of IFC's evaluation systems, which have developed such that IFC is now starting to measure development results across its portfolio of investment and advisory operations. Building on that progress, as discussed in box 1.3, IFC could (in consultation with IEG) advance its metrics to include the wider sector and country-level impacts of its projects and portfolio, and thereby paint a more complete picture of IFC's contribution to development, economic growth, and the improvement of people's lives.

Recommendations

Meeting Stakeholder and Client Needs

Develop a Deeper, More Differentiated Country Approach

Background: IFC has achieved high development success rates through the pursuit of its frontier strategy since 1998, catalyzing investments in high-risk and low-income countries, as well as through investments in strategic sectors. However, IFC does not have a defined strategy in nonfrontier MICs, where most poor people live and where IFC has most of its operations. These countries face a spectrum of private sector development challenges, including a lack of capacity in domestic financial markets and poor infrastructure to support production and trade (see figure 3.1). IFC can play a valuable role in many MICs, even though IFC's additionality in these countries has not always been clear.

While IFC builds up its in-country capacity as part of the decentralization process, the institution has an opportunity to define clearly, at the country level, how it will bring additionality to both the frontier and nonfrontier countries in which it operates.

Recommendation: As IFC decentralizes, it has the opportunity to adopt more tailored country strategies to complement its strong sector and regional approach. This strategy might include, in consultation with the Bank and country govern-ments, the development and pursuit of a set of country-specific private sector development indicators (such as for the level of private, gross, fixed capital formation; banking sector capacity; and private provision of infrastructure).

Place an Emphasis on Rural Development

Background: Economic growth and its resulting market distribution of income matters in reducing the numbers of poor people. IFC may want to acknowledge these elements in its strategic approach, in line with its mission statement. Poverty continues to show a strong rural origin. IFC has not, however, placed much emphasis on rural development in the past. In this regard, evaluation supports a focus on the agribusiness sector, which has had beneficial impacts on farmers and producers through linkage programs, and all instruments to expand access to finance in rural areas. (See box 3.1)

Recommendation: In its country strategies, IFC may consider flagging opportunities to work on the nexus of rural poverty and sustainable natural resources, on which poor people depend, and to identify and develop high-impact agribusiness and rural microfinance projects with widespread demonstration effects, while simultaneously providing leadership in promoting socially and environmentally sustainable practices.

Developing More Seamless World Bank Group Processes

Pursue New Incentives and Mechanisms to Enhance Cooperation with the World Bank in Areas of Synergy

Background: Cooperation with the World Bank in areas of synergy, such as in developing financial markets and infrastructure, has been more modest than anticipated in CASs. While cooperation has been strong in a few countries, it has fallen below expectations in many others. CASs have not proven to be a good basis for enhanced cooperation, and few staff have felt motivated to cooperate across institutional boundaries (see figures 3.2 and 3.3, and table 3.2). Moreover, because of the lack of up-front identification and tracking of investment operations involving IFC–World Bank cooperation, the ultimate development impacts of cooperation are also unclear.

Recommendation: To enhance cooperation with the World Bank in areas of synergy, IFC could (i) consider new incentives and mechanisms to complement the CAS process (with the Bank); and (ii) identify investments at approval that were facilitated by Bank policy or regulatory assistance, and track them throughout the project cycle (through DOTS or other means) in order to judge their success.

Addressing Learning and Growth Needs

Manage the Trade-offs Inherent in the Decentralization Process to Achieve the Highest Possible Work Quality

Background: IFC's strategy predicts greater development impact through higher investment volumes and stronger decentralization. IFC will need to prevent any trade-offs among rapid growth, organizational change, and project execution quality. During a previous period of significant organizational change, 1998–2001, IFC's evaluated supervision quality—a key driver of development success quality and currently at an all-time high—fell sharply (see figure 2.4). The institution has achieved improved quality with decentralization in South Asia (lower market and sponsor risk, higher supervision rates), but with more modest volume growth than in other regions. In addition, IFC may be able to learn from the experiences of the Bank in its efforts to share knowledge across regions and countries

Recommendation: IFC will need to monitor the decentralization process closely to ensure that its work quality remains robust, and support this with a rigorous training program for new investment staff.

Financial and Measurement Issues

Ensure Sound Risk-Management Systems and Develop Risk-Mitigation Products

Background: Experience highlights how quickly financial support for companies can be withdrawn, precipitated by economic or political events. IFC has proved itself a valuable countercyclical investor. One prime example is its support for its large industrial clients in Turkey through periods of market turbulence, and their emergence as major engines of economic growth. Despite the current exuberance in the developing world, IFC should acknowledge in its strategy the threat of a cessation or decline in capital flows to the developing world, its likely impact on clients, and the mitigating actions that would be needed. Planning now to improve risk-management systems, and developing new risk-mitigating products to soften the impact for clients, would strengthen IFC's response to an economic shock and enhance its countercyclical role. (See figure 1.1 and box 3.3.)

Recommendation: IFC will need to make continued efforts to improve its risk-management systems and to prepare for the next correction in the international markets, including perhaps the extended use and development of new risk-mitigation products.

Strengthen the Capacity for Evaluation and Its Application

Background: In recent years, IFC's strategic directions have been increasingly informed by evaluation findings. Substantial progress has occurred in the development of IFC's monitoring and self-evaluation systems, which in the last two years have advanced to where IFC is now starting to measure its development results *across* its portfolio of investment and advisory operations, as well as carry out impact evaluations of its advisory services operations (see box 1.3). IEG will have an important role to play in validating IFC's reported performance under these systems and, building on this progress, in helping IFC advance the measurement of the cumulative effects of its operations and their wider environmental and social impacts. Improved metrics should help IFC structure and manage its operations to further

optimize development effectiveness. Better metrics will allow for deeper performance evaluation and further learning from IFC operations.

Recommendation: As it deepens its self-evaluation and monitoring systems, IFC could, with IEG's assistance, advance its metrics to better understand (and derive lessons about) the wider sector and the country-level impacts of its operations.

APPENDIXES

This appendix explains the methodological approach IEG uses to evaluate the performance of IFC investment operations, as well as the monitoring and self-evaluation framework IFC recently began piloting to assess the results of its advisory operations. The appendix also provides a discussion of the explanatory power of different factors influencing IFC's success rates, and describes the differences between the monitoring and self-evaluation frameworks used by IFC (for its private sector investment operations) and those of the World Bank (for its public sector loan operations).

Methodology for Evaluating IFC Investment Operations

Since 1996, when the present evaluation system was introduced, IEG has rated the development and investment success of IFC investment operations once they reached early operating maturity, generally when operations have recorded at least 18 months of operating revenue, reflected in at least two years of audited financial statements (ex-post evaluation). More recently, since 2004, IEG has assessed the prospects for the future development and investment performance of IFC operations based on the high-risk intensity of IFC-supported projects at approval. IEG is now supplementing the latter (ex-ante) evaluation with a review of business climate trends affecting IFC operations in the years after approval, for operations reaching operating maturity (and to be evaluated) in 2007 and 2008.

Evaluation of Achieved Success Rates

IEG's evaluations of achieved success rates are based on project-level results derived from a system introduced in IFC in 1996, the Expanded Project Supervision Report (XPSR) system. The XPSR process first involves a self-evaluation of a project by an IFC investment department using corporate guidelines. The ratings assigned by investment departments are then independently verified (or rerated) by IEG in terms of bottom-line outcome ratings and their respective subcomponents.

Investments are selected for evaluation on a random sampling basis. Between 1996 and 2006, 627 projects were evaluated under the XPSR system, representing 51 percent coverage of all qualifying investment operations approved over the last decade. Based on a 95 percent confidence interval, the true development success rate of the population of investment operations was between 57 percent and 62 percent (table A1).

Further details of the evaluation framework for IFC investment operations are available on IEG-IFC's website.

Evaluation of Future Success Rates

IEG's evaluation of future success rates involves analysis of key internal and external drivers of past IFC success rates: (i) Project high-risk intensity at approval (internal driver); and (ii) the quality of the business climates that IFC operations are exposed to after approval but before operating maturity (external driver).

To examine project high-risk intensity at approval, IEG assesses whether eight high-risk factors were present or absent at the time of project approval. These high-risk factors are:

- *Sponsor quality*—the sponsor's experience, financial capacity, commitment to the project, and business reputation;

Table A1. Sample of Evaluated Operations, 1996–2006 (in percents)

Indicator	Success rate in the sampled evaluated operations,	Estimate of success rate in the population of operations,	Standard error	Sampling error	95% confidence interval	
					Lower bound	Upper bound
Project development rating	59	59	1	3	57	62
IFC investment return	56	56	1	3	53	59
IFC's work quality	66	66	1	3	64	69

Source: IEG.

- *Product market*—market distortions or having no clear, inherent, competitive advantage and risk;
- *Debt service burden*—the burden of servicing a debt in the year when principal repayments start;
- *Project type*—greenfield projects (building on previously undeveloped land) generally involve higher risks than expansions;
- *Sector risk*—sectors exposed to high price or supply volatility (such as agribusiness), or weather and safety conditions (such as tourism) are higher risk, as demonstrated in IFC's investment experience;
- *Country business climate at project approval*—IEG uses the Wall Street Journal/Heritage Foundation's Index of Economic Freedom—Overall Synthesis Ratings as the primary indicator of a country's business climate quality;
- *IFC review intensity*—projects that do not go to the Credit Department for review or to the Corporate Investment Committee are considered to be higher risk; and
- *Nonrepeat project*—IFC's first-time clients are generally higher risk.

IEG began its profiling of high-risk factors in 2004, in response to a 2003 request by the Board of Directors for IEG to assess whether IFC's structural and process improvements during 1998– 2001—such as the establishment of a Credit Department and Portfolio Units—had resulted in higher IFC success rates in its operations. At the time, IEG profiled 259 "mature" operations (operations that had been self-evaluated and the ratings of which IEG had validated) and 259 "new" operations (operations approved since the completion of various IFC quality steps in 2003 and 2004). This profiling has evolved to the point where IEG has now risk-profiled 388 "mature" operations, which were evaluated in the last six years (approved during 1995–2000) as well as a random sample of "new" operations (290 in number) approved between 2002 and 2005.

For each operation, IEG profiles the operation's high-risk intensity according to appraisal information available at project approval. Because of the diverse nature of these projects, IEG does not assign weights to these risk factors. The analysis focuses on a project's intrinsic high-risk intensity at approval, which, as the analysis in the main report shows, strongly influences their development impact quality, and accordingly reflects some, but not all, elements of IFC quality-at-entry (such as the intensity of IFC credit review at appraisal but not the quality of transaction structuring).

To assess business climate trends after approval (but before operating maturity), IEG reviews the change in the level of country credit risk, as measured by the *Institutional Investor* Country Credit Risk ratings, that IFC operations are exposed to, following their approval and up until the most recent date for which ratings are available. Because of inherent uncertainty in global and emerging market conditions, which can have material impacts on country credit risk ratings, IEG has limited its review of business climate trends to two years ahead of the current evaluation sample; in this case, to operations that will be evaluated in 2007 and 2008 (and which were approved in 2002 and 2003).

The *Institutional Investor* ratings were first compiled in 1979, and are now published in March and September of every year, for an increasing number of countries (174 countries in 2006). The ratings are numerical, ranging from 0 to 100, with 100 corresponding to the lowest chance of sovereign default on its foreign currency debts. The *Institutional Investor* relies on evaluations, provided by economists and international banks, of the creditworthiness of the countries to be rated, with respondents using their own criteria. Responses are aggregated by the *Institutional Investor,* with greater weights being given to responses from institutions with higher worldwide exposure.

Methodology for Evaluating IFC Advisory Services Operations

In 2006, IFC started to introduce a systematic approach to evaluating its advisory services operations. To date, IFC has completed two evaluation pilots, involving 300 advisory operations. IFC is expected to report its ratings for these operations in its annual report in October 2007, with IEG presenting its independent assessment of these ratings in the *Report on Operations Evaluation, 2007.*

The evaluation framework covers the following areas of performance of IFC's advisory services operations, with an indication of what equates to satisfactory performance in each area:

- *Strategic relevance.* Assistance addressed major priority issues to a large extent; was appropriate for conditions at initiation and completion; and achieved a majority of intended cost recovery.
- *Efficiency.* Assistance had a positive cost-benefit ratio; resources used to provide assistance were expended economically; and resources used were reasonable in relation to alternatives.
- *Output achievement.* Most of the major outputs were achieved.

- *Outcome achievement.* Clients were satisfied with the assistance; most of the major outcomes were achieved; areas for improvement in environmental and social conditions were communicated to the client, with some improvements made or ongoing.
- *Impact achievement.* Most intended impacts on the direct recipient(s) were achieved; some impact beyond the direct recipient(s).

In addition to the above five performance areas, IEG will also rate IFC's work quality and the work quality of consultants or others involved (client and/or stakeholders) in the operation.

Explanatory Power of Different Influences on IFC Development Peformance

The factors that drive the development impact quality of IFC investment operations, as described in chapter 2, broadly explain about two-thirds of IFC's results. When two or more of the following variables are present—country risk migration, from high risk to non-high risk, between approval and evaluation; fewer than four high-risk factors; high IFC work quality; and an investment in a strategic sector (infrastructure, financial interests, or health and education)—the development rating for the operation is positive 68 percent of the time.

A project-level econometric investigation of the determinants of IFC success rates, based on data from 388 operations evaluated during the 2000–05 period, reveals that IFC work quality is the strongest determinant of the development and investment performance of IFC-supported projects. Individual independent (or explanatory) variables with high significance were: positive or negative changes in country credit risk (measured by the Institutional Investor); project type (greenfield or expansion); sector risk; sponsor quality; product market risk; nonrepeat risk; whether the investment was in a strategic sector; and each of the component elements of IFC work quality (appraisal quality; supervision quality; IFC role and contribution). All variables, with the exception of changes in country credit risk (measured on a continuous scale), were rated on a binary scale,

Figure A1. World Bank and IFC Evaluate Operations at Different Stages

▶ IFC and the World Bank share the same mission of poverty reduction but follow different business models in pursuit of this mission. Their project cycles accordingly differ, with IFC's project cycle ending at full repayment (in the case of a loan) or equity divestment, and with the Bank's cycle ending at or around project implementation.

Bank:

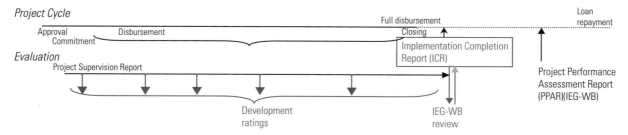

IFC:

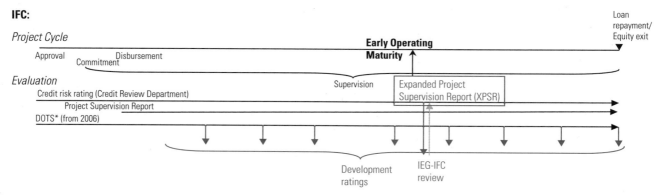

Source: IEG.

*Development Outcome Tracking System

with 1 denoting high risk or present (in the case of strategic sector choice) and 0 as non-high risk, or absent (in the case of strategic sector choice). The analysis was carried out using Probit analysis, with significance determined on the basis of "z" values. We also checked for multicollinearity among the explanatory variables and found none.

Differences between IFC and World Bank Evaluation Frameworks

IFC and the World Bank share the same mission of poverty reduction, but follow different busi-ness models in pursuit of this mission. As the re-port discusses, IFC generally works with the pri-vate sector (and in some cases with governments, for instance, in the area of business climate diag-nostics and development), while the Bank provides its products and services to governments. Ac-cordingly, the supervision, monitoring, and eval-uation systems that each institution uses are different. As the chart above illustrates, IFC's proj-ect cycle ends with full repayment (of a loan) or equity divestment, while the Bank's cycle ends at or around project implementation (figure A1).

APPENDIX B: PERFORMANCE OF IFC-SUPPORTED PROJECTS
              AND THE PROFITABILITY OF IFC INVESTMENT OPERATIONS:
              FURTHER ANALYSIS

The following tables and figures present further disaggregation of the development, investment, and work quality ratings of IFC-supported projects. In turn, they show:

- Rating trends (figure B1) and characteristics (table B1) of IFC-supported projects, by subindicator, between 1996 and 2006;
- Characteristics of IFC-supported projects, by subindicator, in the last three years, 2004–06 (table B2);

- Trends in development ratings of IFC-supported projects, by region, between 1996 and 2006 (figure B2);
- Development rating trends of IFC-supported projects, by industry department, between 1996 and 2006 (figure B3); and
- Combined development and investment success rates and characteristics of IFC-supported projects, between 1996 and 2006 (figure B4).

Figure B1.   Rating Trends of IFC-Supported Projects, by Development Outcome, Investment Return, and Work Quality, 1996–2006

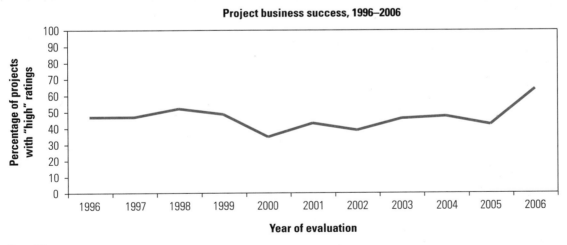

Source: IEG.

(Figure continues on next page)

Figure B1. Rating Trends of IFC-Supported Projects, by Development Outcome, Investment Return, and Work Quality, 1996–2006 *(continued)*

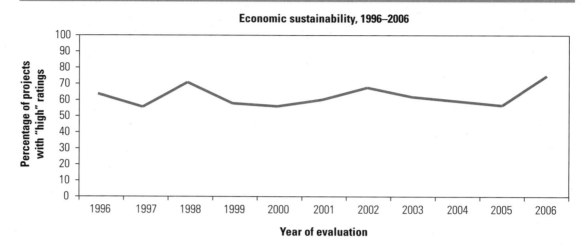

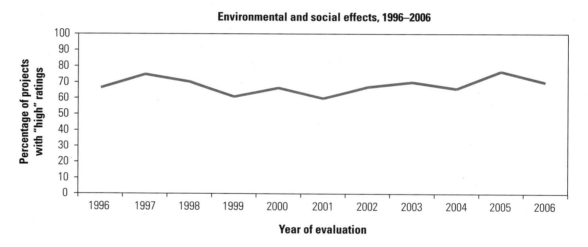

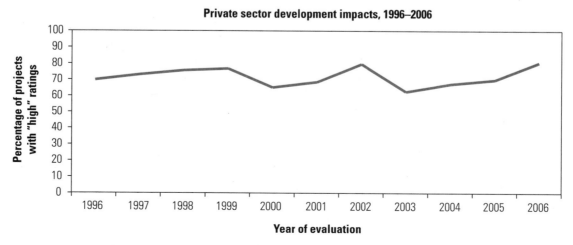

Source: IEG.

Figure B1. Rating Trends of IFC-Supported Projects, by Development Outcome, Investment Return, and Work Quality, 1996–2006 *(continued)*

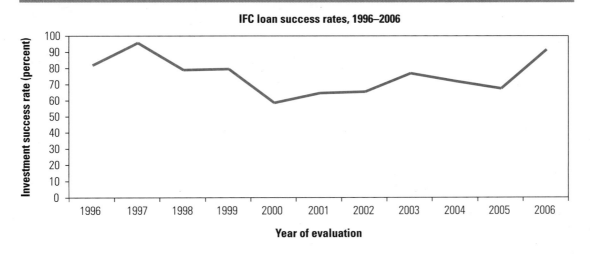

IFC loan success rates, 1996–2006

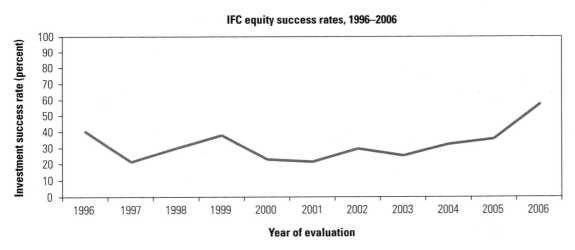

IFC equity success rates, 1996–2006

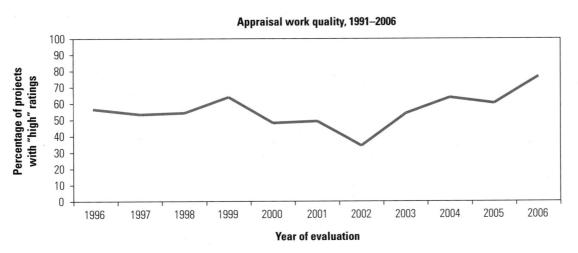

Appraisal work quality, 1991–2006

Source: IEG.

(Figure continues on next page)

Figure B1. Rating Trends of IFC-Supported Projects, by Development Outcome, Investment Return, and Work Quality, 1996–2006 *(continued)*

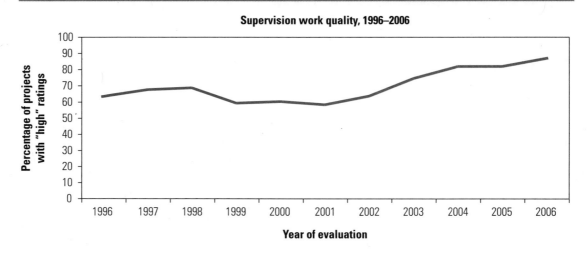

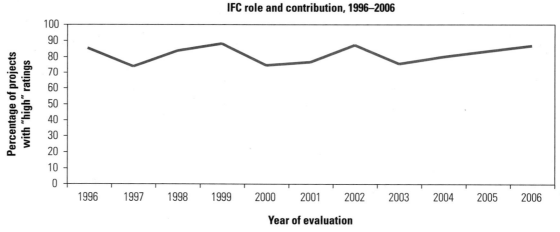

Source: IEG.

Table B1. Characteristics of High and Low Development, Investment Return, and Work Quality Ratings, by Subindicator, 1996–2006 (in percents)

		LOW			HIGH		
		Highly unsuccessful	Unsuccessful	Mostly unsuccessful	Mostly successful	Successful	Highly Successful

Development ratings, 1996–2006

DEVELOPMENT RATING	7	16	18	21	28	10
	41			59		
(by commitment volume)	6	13	16	24	31	10
	35			65		

	Unsatisfactory	Partly unsatisfactory	Satisfactory	Excellent
Project business success	35	19	22	24
	54		46	
Economic sustainability	21	18	40	22
	38		62	
Environmental effects	6	26	56	12
	33		67	
Private sector development	8	20	45	26
	28		72	

IFC investment return ratings, 1996–2006

	Unsatisfactory	Partly unsatisfactory	Satisfactory	Excellent
IFC INVESTMENT RETURN	33	11	42	14
	44		56	
(by commitment volume)	25	13	47	15
	38		62	
Loan	17	9	67	7
	26		74	
Equity	57	12	10	21
	69		31	

IFC work quality ratings, 1996–2006

	Unsatisfactory	Partly unsatisfactory	Satisfactory	Excellent
IFC WORK QUALITY	8	26	54	12
	34		66	
(by commitment volume)	6	20	58	15
	26		74	
Screening, appraisal, structuring	13	32	43	12
	45		55	
Supervision and administration	5	27	52	16
	32		68	
Role and contribution	7	12	54	27
	19		81	

Source: IEG.

Note: (i) Following a similar approach since 1996, IEG uses a binary interpretation of these evaluation results, which describes operation ratings as either "high" or "low." The central dividing line in the above tables separates the two categories.

(ii) By-volume figures are the percentages of the total committed IFC investment amounts in each outcome-rating group.

(iii) The success rates above are the percentages of all assigned ratings.

Table B2. Characteristics of High and Low Development, Investment Return, and Work Quality Ratings, by Subindicator, 2004–06 (in percents)

	LOW			HIGH		
	Highly unsuccessful	Unsuccessful	Mostly unsuccessful	Mostly successful	Successful	Highly Successful
Development ratings, 1996–2006						
DEVELOPMENT RATING	*8*	*17*	*19*	*18*	*31*	*7*
	44			*56*		
(by commitment volume)	*4*	*14*	*16*	*22*	*38*	*5*
	35			*65*		
	Unsatisfactory		Partly unsatisfactory	Satisfactory		Excellent
Project business success	34		16	28		22
	50			50		
Economic sustainability	19		19	42		20
	38			62		
Environmental effects	8		22	63		8
	29			71		
Private sector development	6		22	47		25
	28			72		

	Unsatisfactory		Partly unsatisfactory	Satisfactory		Excellent
IFC investment return ratings, 1996–2006						
IFC INVESTMENT RETURN	*30*		*9*	*44*		*18*
	39			*61*		
(by commitment volume)	*18*		*10*	*54*		*18*
	28			*72*		
Loan	16		8	67		9
	24			76		
Equity	48		13	10		30
	60			40		

	Unsatisfactory		Partly unsatisfactory	Satisfactory		Excellent
IFC work quality ratings, 1996–2006						
IFC WORK QUALITY	*2*		*22*	*63*		*13*
	23			*77*		
(by commitment volume)	*4*		*12*	*66*		*17*
	16			*83*		
Screening, appraisal, structuring	6		31	51		12
	37			63		
Supervision and administration	0		18	62		20
	18			82		
Role and contribution	3		15	52		30
	18			82		

Source: IEG.

Note: (i) Following a similar approach since 1996, IEG uses a binary interpretation of these evaluation results, which describes operation ratings as either "high" or "low." The central dividing line in the above tables separates the two categories.

(ii) By-volume figures are the percentages of the total committed IFC investment amounts in each outcome-rating group.

(iii) The success rates above are the percentages of all assigned ratings.

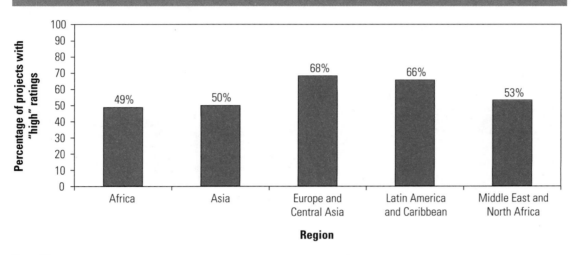

Figure B2. Development Ratings of IFC-Supported Projects, by Region, 1996–2006

Source: IEG.

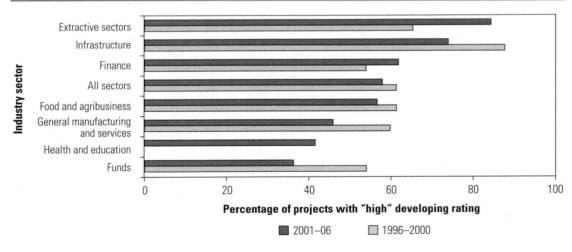

Figure B3. Development Rating Trends of IFC-Supported Projects, by Industry Department, 1996–2006

Source: IEG.

Figure B4. Combined Development and Investment Ratings and Characteristics of IFC Operations, 1996–2006

▶ A comparison of the characteristics of investment operations in each of the four ratings groups reveals the following:

- Operations with *high-high* ratings (square 1) featured high work quality in 91 percent of cases, compared with 24 percent in operations with *low-low* ratings (square 4). High development ratings (squares 1 and 2) featured high work quality in 89 percent of cases.

- Operations with high development ratings (squares 1 and 2) featured a very high proportion (78 percent) of environmentally compliant projects, as compared with operations with low development ratings (squares 3 and 4).

- There is significant variation in IFC's choice of investment instrument across the four ratings combinations:

  ○ Square 1: *High-high* ratings have tended to feature loan and/or equity investments in almost the same proportions as exist in the overall portfolio, at a ratio of 2:1, loan to equity, respectively. There is, therefore, nothing unusual about *high-high* ratings in terms of IFC instrument mix.

  ○ Square 2: In 87 percent of evaluated operations that achieved high development ratings but low investment returns, IFC had invested equity. In most cases, investments in this square were made in businesses that had better-than-average project returns, have continued trading, and have therefore succeeded in generating at least minimally satisfactory project development impacts.

IFC's equity returns have nevertheless been impaired by factors such as illiquidity, weak exit mechanisms, and/or currency crises that have eroded U.S. dollar valuations. While few of these investments have therefore yielded losses for IFC, their returns have been less than satisfactory.

○ Square 3: 94 percent of operations categorized as having achieved high investment ratings but low development ratings featured straight loan investments. In these cases, the underlying projects have not, themselves, been sufficiently profitable (their project business success rate was only 6 percent) and, consequently, have yielded little in the way of economic or social benefits, and/or may have featured material environmental performance shortfalls. Despite this, IFC has received repayment of its loan by virtue of its ranking claim on company cashflow and the collateral security package. Also, the project's sponsor may have decided, for strategic reasons, to advance funds to the enterprise from its own resources, thus keeping the business alive and repaying its lenders.

○ Square 4: *Low-low* ratings were substantially overweighted in equity investments compared with *high-high* ratings, and the success rate and aggregate returns of these operations were well below average. These returns did not compensate for the projects' materially higher-than-average risk intensity—country, sector, sponsor, and market risk were highest for projects in this square. These operations also featured the lowest level of satisfactory or above (that is, "high") IFC work quality (24 percent), including IFC's additionality through its role and contribution.

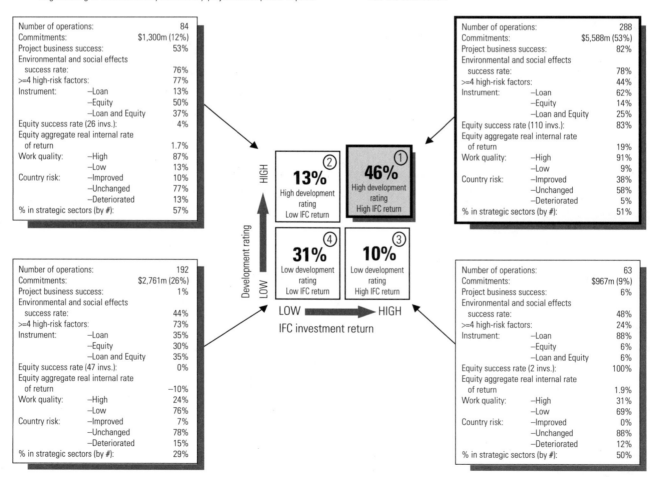

Number of operations:		84
Commitments:		$1,300m (12%)
Project business success:		53%
Environmental and social effects success rate:		76%
>=4 high-risk factors:		77%
Instrument:	—Loan	13%
	—Equity	50%
	—Loan and Equity	37%
Equity success rate (26 invs.):		4%
Equity aggregate real internal rate of return		1.7%
Work quality:	—High	87%
	—Low	13%
Country risk:	—Improved	10%
	—Unchanged	77%
	—Deteriorated	13%
% in strategic sectors (by #):		57%

Number of operations:		288
Commitments:		$5,588m (53%)
Project business success:		82%
Environmental and social effects success rate:		78%
>=4 high-risk factors:		44%
Instrument:	—Loan	62%
	—Equity	14%
	—Loan and Equity	25%
Equity success rate (110 invs.):		83%
Equity aggregate real internal rate of return		19%
Work quality:	—High	91%
	—Low	9%
Country risk:	—Improved	38%
	—Unchanged	58%
	—Deteriorated	5%
% in strategic sectors (by #):		51%

② 13% High development rating Low IFC return

① 46% High development rating High IFC return

④ 31% Low development rating Low IFC return

③ 10% Low development rating High IFC return

HIGH / LOW — Development rating

LOW → HIGH — IFC investment return

Number of operations:		192
Commitments:		$2,761m (26%)
Project business success:		1%
Environmental and social effects success rate:		44%
>=4 high-risk factors:		73%
Instrument:	—Loan	35%
	—Equity	30%
	—Loan and Equity	35%
Equity success rate (47 invs.):		0%
Equity aggregate real internal rate of return		−10%
Work quality:	—High	24%
	—Low	76%
Country risk:	—Improved	7%
	—Unchanged	78%
	—Deteriorated	15%
% in strategic sectors (by #):		29%

Number of operations:		63
Commitments:		$967m (9%)
Project business success:		6%
Environmental and social effects success rate:		48%
>=4 high-risk factors:		24%
Instrument:	—Loan	88%
	—Equity	6%
	—Loan and Equity	6%
Equity success rate (2 invs.):		100%
Equity aggregate real internal rate of return		1.9%
Work quality:	—High	31%
	—Low	69%
Country risk:	—Improved	0%
	—Unchanged	88%
	—Deteriorated	12%
% in strategic sectors (by #):		50%

IFC Profitability from Investment Operations, 1996–2006

To supplement IEG's evaluations of achieved success rates (ex-post evaluation) and expected success rates (ex-ante evaluation), IEG also reviews the profitability of IFC's whole portfolio of investment operations. IEG carries out this analysis to discern patterns that may have an effect on IFC's development performance, given the close connection between investment and development success. Figure B5 sets out the trends in the profitability of IFC investment operations since 1996, by loan and equity instrument, and table B3 shows the profitability of IFC investment operations for the whole of period 1996–2006.

Figure B5. Net Profitability of IFC Investment Operations, FY96–FY06

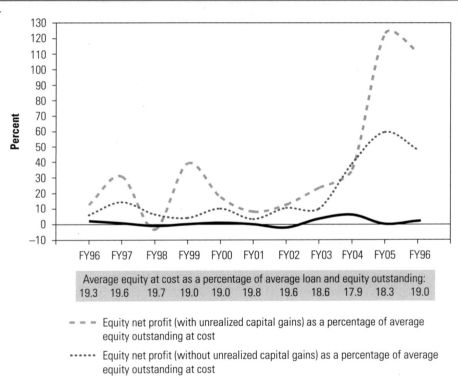

Average equity at cost as a percentage of average loan and equity outstanding:
19.3 19.6 19.7 19.0 19.0 19.8 19.6 18.6 17.9 18.3 19.0

- - -   Equity net profit (with unrealized capital gains) as a percentage of average equity outstanding at cost

......   Equity net profit (without unrealized capital gains) as a percentage of average equity outstanding at cost

——   Loan net profit as a percentage of average loan outstanding

Source: Profitability analysis is derived from IFC annual financial reports and internal IFC databases.

Note: Excludes income from IFC Treasury Department operations. The average outstanding balance for a fiscal year is the average of the outstanding amount at the beginning and the end of the fiscal year.

Table B3. IFC Net Profitability Contribution of Investment Operations (as a percentage of average outstanding balance)

	Average FY96–FY06 (percent)
Average loan outstanding	**100**
Average income from loans (interest and fees)	7.5
Average loan loss provisions	1.2
Average cost of funds after swap effects	3.0
Average administrative expenses	1.9
Loan net profitability rate	**1.4**
Average equity outstanding at cost	**100**
Average dividend income	7.0
Average realized capital gains on sold/closed investments	13.2
Active investments:	
Valuation at end-of-period	156.0
Original cost of shares held at end-of-period	101.7
Average unrealized gains on active investments	**53.6**
Average administrative expenses	2.5
Equity net profitability rate	**71.3**
Average equity at cost as a percentage of loan + equity at cost	**22.1**
Combined IFC Loan and equity net profitability rate	**16.9**

Source: Profitability analysis is derived from IFC annual financial reports and internal IFC databases.

Note: Excludes income from IFC Treasury Department operations. The average outstanding balance for a fiscal year is the average of the outstanding amount at the beginning and the end of the fiscal year.

APPENDIX C: DEFINITIONS OF EVALUATION TERMS

INVESTMENT OPERATIONS

Company   The entity implementing the project and, generally, IFC's investment counterparty. For financial markets operations, it refers to the financial intermediary as distinct from its portfolio of IFC-financed sub-project companies.

Investment   IFC's financing instrument(s) in the evaluated operation, such as a loan, guarantee, equity, and underwriting commitment.

Operation   IFC's objectives, activities, and results in making and administering its investment.

Project   The company objectives, capital investments, funding program, and related business activities being partially financed by IFC's investment selected for evaluation.

For example, for one *operation*, IFC provided $55 million for the company's $100 million cement manufacturing expansion *project* in the form of a $20 million A-loan, a $30 million B-loan from commercial banks, and a $5 million equity *investment*.

Financial markets   All projects where the company is a financial intermediary or financial services company, including agency lines.

Nonfinancial markets   All other projects, except collective investment vehicles (investment funds); sometimes referred to as "real sector" projects.

Development rating   The development result(s) of an IFC-supported project, assessed in four respects: project business success; economic sustainability; environmental and social effects; and wider private sector development impacts.

Project business success   For real sector projects, such success is measured by the project's financial rate of return (FRR), as compared with the company's cost of capital. For financial sector projects, success is measured by the positive contributions of the associated sub-portfolios or asset growth to the intermediary's profitability, financial condition, and business objectives.

Economic sustainability	Measured, where possible, by the project's economic rate of return (ERR), as compared with a minimum benchmark of 10 percent. This indicator takes into account net gains or losses by nonfinanciers, nonquantifiable impacts, and contributions to widely held development objectives.
Environmental and social effects	The degree to which a project meets IFC's environmental, social, health and safety requirements at approval; and policies, guidelines, and standards that would apply if the project were appraised today.
Wider PSD impacts	A project's private sector development impact beyond the project company, particularly its demonstration effect in creating a sustainable enterprise capable of attracting finance, increasing competition, and establishing linkages.
Development success	Based on performance in these four dimensions, the IFC-supported project was rated overall as having a high-quality development result.
Development effectiveness	The aggregation of project development results at the country, sector, theme, regional, and global levels.
IFC investment return rating	An assessment of the gross profit contribution quality of an IFC loan and/or equity investment (without taking into account transaction costs or the cost of IFC equity capital).
	Loans are rated satisfactory provided they are expected to be repaid in full, with interest and fees as scheduled (or are prepaid or rescheduled without loss).
	Equities are rated satisfactory if they yield an appropriate premium on the return on a loan to the same company.

NON-INVESTMENT OPERATIONS: Advisory services (could include technical assistance components)

Outcomes	Implementation of recommendations or advice.
Impacts	Changes that occurred following the implementation of a recommendation.

For example, an operation recommends that a country amend its leasing law to incorporate best practice in the region. The *outcome* is the country amends the leasing law in line with the recommendation. The *impact* is the leasing industry becomes attractive to potential sponsors, leading to the establishment of new companies after the amendment of the leasing law.

ENDNOTES

Executive Summary

1. IEG changed its name from the Operations Evaluation Group in 2006.

2. As determined by having an Institutional Country Credit Risk rating of less than 30.

3. Generally, when operations have recorded at least 18 months of operating revenue.

4. The two institutions accordingly employ different evaluation frameworks, including in terms of focus, timing of evaluation, and benchmarks. For example, the World Bank evaluates projects immediately after disbursement while IFC does so a few years after disbursement (at early operating maturity). The Bank assesses results based on achievement of objectives, while IFC considers financial and economic results based on market benchmarks, along with environmental and social impacts, and private sector impacts beyond the project company.

5. IFC 2006b.

6. Middle-income countries that are non-high risk, meaning they have an Institutional Country Credit Risk rating greater than 30.

7. *Cooperation* is defined broadly to include any interaction among World Bank Group institutions aimed at improving the development impact of World Bank Group instruments by maximizing synergies and reducing duplication and inconsistencies. It includes both *coordination* (efforts to integrate the strategies of the two institutions to accomplish common objectives, such as through division of labor, but which does not typically involve interaction on specific interventions) and *collaboration* (defined as interaction between the two institutions on specific interventions).

Résumé analytique

1. Le Groupe d'évaluation des opérations (OED) est devenu le Groupe indépendant d'évaluation en 2006.

2. Indiqué par l'attribution par l'institution d'une note de risque-pays inférieure à 30.

3. Généralement, lorsque les opérations ont généré des recettes d'exploitation pendant au moins 18 mois.

4. Les deux institutions emploient de ce fait des cadres d'évaluation différents, notamment en ce qui concerne le ciblage, le calendrier d'évaluation et les valeurs de référence. Par exemple, la Banque mondiale évalue les projets immédiatement après le décaissement du financement tandis que l'IFC le fait plusieurs années après le décaissement (une fois que le projet a atteint son rythme de croisière). La Banque évalue les résultats sur la base de la réalisation des objectifs, tandis que l'IFC examine les résultats financiers et économiques sur la base des références du marché, de même que les impacts environnementaux et sociaux et les impacts sur le secteur privé qui sortent du cadre de l'entreprise du projet.

5. IFC 2006b

6. Les pays à revenu intermédiaire qui ne posent pas de risques élevés, c'est-à-dire ceux qui ont une note de risque-pays supérieure à 30.

7. La *coopération* est définie au sens large comme toute interaction entre les institutions du Groupe de la Banque mondiale visant à améliorer l'impact sur le développement des instruments du Groupe de la Banque mondiale en optimisant les synergies et en réduisant les chevauchements et les incohérences. Elle recouvre aussi bien la *coordination* (efforts visant à intégrer les stratégies des deux institutions en vue d'atteindre des objectifs communs tels que la division du travail, mais qui n'implique pas le plus souvent d'interactions dans le cadre d'interventions particulières) que la *collaboration* (définie comme les interactions entre les deux institutions dans le cadre d'interventions particulières).

Resumen

1. El GEI cambió su nombre anterior, Departamento de Evaluación de Operaciones, en 2006.

2. Según determina su calificación *Institutional Country Credit Risk* de menos de 30.

3. Por lo general, cuando las operaciones registraron al menos 18 meses de ingresos operativos.

4. Las dos instituciones utilizan distintos marcos de evaluación, incluso en términos de foco, momento de evaluación y puntos de referencia. Por ejemplo, el Banco Mundial evalúa los proyectos inmediatamente luego de los desembolsos, mientras que la IFC lo hace unos años después de los desembolsos (al inicio de la madurez operacional). El Banco analiza los resultados basándose en el cumplimiento de los objetivos, mientras que la IFC considera los resultados financieros y económicos sobre la base de los puntos de referencia del mercado, junto con los impactos sociales y ambientales y los impactos del sector privado más allá de la empresa del proyecto.

5. IFC 2006b.

6. Los países de ingreso mediano que no tienen altos riesgos, lo que significa que tienen una calificación *Institutional Country Credit Risk* superior a 30.

7. Definida en términos amplios, la *cooperación* incluye cualquier interacción entre las instituciones del Grupo del Banco Mundial dirigida a mejorar el impacto en términos de desarrollo de los instrumentos del Banco Mundial, maximizando las sinergias y reduciendo la duplicación y las inconsistencias. Abarca tanto la *coordinación* (los esfuerzos para integrar las estrategias de las dos instituciones a fin de alcanzar objetivos comunes, por ejemplo a través de la división del trabajo, pero que generalmente no implican la interacción en las intervenciones específicas) como la *colaboración* (que se define como la interacción entre las dos instituciones en las intervenciones específicas).

Chapter 1

1. Before 1996, IEG evaluated IFC's project performance using Investment Appraisal Reports. In 1996, a systematic system for evaluating IFC's development and investment results was introduced, the Expanded Project Supervision Report (XPSR) System.

2. Prior to 2006, a number of program-level evaluations were carried out, including an evaluation of four small and medium enterprise facilities in 2004, and an evaluation of foreign investment advisory services in 1998.

3. World Bank forthcoming.

4. This figure includes International Bank for Reconstruction and Development gross disbursements of about $232 billion and International Development Association gross disbursements of about $110 billion, but does not include the cost of trust funds. Except for a spike between 1997 and 1999, International Bank for Reconstruction and Development lending volumes fell between 1991 and 2006 (from $16 billion to $14 billion per year), while International Development Association volumes increased over the same period, from around $6 billion to $9 billion per year.

5. See IEG-IFC 2006b.

6. Determined using the Atlas Method, as of 2004.

7. Total project funding, including donor contributions.

8. Unless specifically noted, IEG means IEG-IFC in this document.

9. While the rating seeks to examine what would have happened without the project, there are limitations to this judgment, in the sense that there is imperfect information about other sources of financing available to clients, and about the opportunity cost, in development terms, to IFC of investing in one operation and not another.

10. The fixed loan interest rate is either the actual interest rate of a fixed-rate loan, the fixed-rate equivalent of an actual variable loan, or the notional interest rate IFC would have charged to a similar company in the same country.

11. For example, the World Bank evaluates projects right after disbursement while IFC does so a few years after disbursement (at early operating maturity). The Bank assesses results based on achievement of objectives while IFC considers financial and economic results based on market benchmarks, along with environmental and social impacts as well as private sector impacts beyond the project company.

12. IFC has twice strengthened its environmental and social effects requirements for projects in the past 10 years. In 1998, IFC's Environmental and Social Review of Projects came into force in conjunction with the new *World Bank Group Safeguard Policies* and the *1998 Pollution Prevention and Abatement Handbook*, which in-

cluded many updated technical guidelines. The latest update to IFC environmental and social effects requirements took place in 2006, when the Board of Directors approved new Policy and Performance Standards, and a new Environmental and Social Review of Projects.

13. IFC made its very first investments in Chad and Armenia in 2000.

14. Individual evaluations suggest that IFC adopted a speculative approach to its investments in the Internet sector at this time, investing relatively small amounts of equity in start-up companies, with minimal follow-up supervision. IFC was not alone in this strategy and, in common with many other investors and venture capitalists, suffered losses on those investments with the bursting of the technology sector bubble.

15. In the 1995–2000 approval period, 388 operations were profiled; and in the 2002–05 approval period, 290 operations.

16. Average high-risk intensity fell from 4.00 in 1995, to 3.16 in 2005. Excluding country risk, high-risk intensity declined from 3.35 in 1995, to 2.34 in 2005.

17. This pattern is consistent with the population of projects from which the 2007 sample was derived, with 43 percent of high-risk country approvals showing an improvement in their country risk ratings since approval in 2002.

18. Among the population of projects from which the 2008 evaluation sample will be drawn, 40 percent of high-risk country approvals have shown an improvement in their country risk ratings since approval in 2003.

19. The correlation between investment ratings and environmental and social effects ratings is weaker than the correlation between investment ratings and the other development ratings, although the correlation is strong at the margins, where investment success is rated as unsatisfactory.

20. See IFC 2005.

21. IFC 2006a.

22. IFC's own credit review ratings trend downward between project approval and early operating maturity, but stabilize from early operating maturity onward. A comparison of expected equity returns at evaluation during the 2002–04 period, with realized rates of return on equity at exit (carried out for the *FY2005 Annual Review of Evaluation Findings in IFC*), shows that, overall, 84 percent of the ratings IEG assigned in 2002–04 would remain unchanged.

23. Between 1996 and 2005, IFC's evaluated success rates in EBRD countries were as follows: 63 percent of operations had high development ratings, 50 percent had high investment ratings, while 75 percent had high work-quality ratings. EBRD does not disaggregate its performance in this way. Instead, it reports an overall success rate of 57 percent between 1996 and 2005. See EBRD projects database at http://www.ebrd.com/projects/eval/method.htm.

24. EBRD considers projects to be ready for evaluation after at least 12 months of operations with 1 year of audited financials, whereas IFC requires 18 months of operations, reflected in at least 2 years of audited financials.

25. This evaluation approach has been extended to country, corporate, sector, thematic, and global policy evaluations, by making suitable adjustments to the criteria.

Chapter 2

1. During this time, IEG produced some 50 macro evaluation reports with over 1,000 findings and recommendations. IEG also delivered 808 micro evaluations: 627 Evaluation Notes—independent validations of XPSRs, covering the results of IFC's investment operations—and 181 Project Completion Report Reviews—independent validations of Project Completion Reports, covering the results of IFC's advisory services operations.

2. Out of 22 evaluated operations in conflict-affected countries (defined as countries with an ongoing conflict at the time of project approval, or a conflict in the three years preceding approval), 64 percent achieved high development success, which is actually marginally higher than the 59-percent average of the rest of IFC.

3. For more detail, see IEG 2004.

4. The private operator introduced new technology and know-how and achieved a 234 percent increase in productivity over a five-year period, increasing container moves from 80,000 a year, to over 300,000, well ahead of forecasts.

5. IEG-IFC 2007.

6. See, for example, IEG-IFC 2006a.

7. This finding is reported in previous IEG-IFC annual reviews of IFC performance.

8. IEG-IFC forthcoming(b).

9. World Bank 2005.

10. In 2005, a new management team, with new control procedures and a refocused business model, was introduced at the African Management Services Company; and the African Project Development Facility was replaced by the Private Enterprise Partnership for Africa. PEP-Africa has a broader mandate than APDF, and covers multiyear, sector-focused efforts based on three pillars: (i) building SME capacity; (ii) improving business climates (to reduce administrative barriers, regulatory costs and other costs of doing business); and (iii) facilitating downstream IFC investments. The strategy envisages working in close partnership to integrate IFC sector expertise with the PSD investment climate and the SME development expertise of the World Bank Group. It is expected to mobilize donor funding to three times that of IFC funding—leading to total funding of about $160 million between 2006 and 2010.

11. IEG 2006.

12. IFC's administrative expenses in Sub-Saharan Africa were 4.2 percent of average investment outstanding, compared with 2.2 percent in the rest of IFC.

13. As evidenced in a higher proportion of projects exhibiting high-risk intensity, according to IEG-IFC's project risk profiling.

14. Often, the foreign, committed sponsor brings resources and skills to raise the environmental and social effects capacity of its local partner but, also, locally owned and managed companies have been committed to building strong environmental management capacity, especially if they export to markets with strict environmental requirements.

15. IEG-IFC forthcoming(b).

16. A proposed project is deemed to be in category A if it is likely to have significant adverse environmental impacts that are sensitive, diverse, or unprecedented. These projects may affect an area broader than the sites or facilities subject to physical works. A proposed project is classified in category B if its potential adverse environmental impacts on human populations or environmentally important areas—including wetlands, forests, grasslands, and other natural habitats—are less adverse than those of category-A projects.

17. Other steps include developing the environmental management capacity in FIs that are not accustomed to appraising and supervising their subprojects from an environmental and social effects perspective. This has been a challenge for IFC. Therefore, the new Environmental and Social Reporting Procedures introduced in 2006 demand substantial engagement during appraisal and capacity building for FIs with environmentally risky portfolios. The Sustainable Financial Markets facility to establish FI capacity began implementation in 2003–04, and the results from this initiative are not yet fully evident. A one-stop training facility (Competitive Business Advance) was closed in 2006 because one-stop training was insufficient for long-term capacity building. IFC plans to roll out environmental and social effects training in the regions over time, but as a permanent offering through a training partner. IFC will invest in the partner's capacity; currently the India and China regional partnerships are under way and four or five other partnerships are planned for 2008. This will, however, not reach all IFC clients immediately. Therefore, in 2008, the Competitive Business Advance will be turned into a Web-based e-learning module for any client with Internet access to obtain the training. Additionally, various tools such as a Web-based platform will be developed to further support client capacity creation.

18. See, for example, IEG-IFC 2005b and 2006a.

19. See IEG-IFC 2006b,

20. The fund will begin as a pilot program, with an initial capitalization of $30 million, which is expected to facilitate between $100 million and $200 million of local currency loans (see IFC 2007).

21. IEG-IFC forthcoming(c).

22. IEG-IFC forthcoming(a).

23. IEG-IFC forthcoming(c).

24. These recommendations are being implemented by IFC Management, through the establishment of the Development Effectiveness Unit in 2005, and the subsequent introduction of a Development Outcome Tracking System, as well as the introduction of Long-Term Performance Awards for delivery of operations with high development effectiveness.

Chapter 3

1. This was the so-called "proactive" scenario. Under a more reactive scenario, IFC expected its approvals to increase by about 50 percent, to $4.5 billion by 2005.

2. Between 1996 and 2006, the number of IFC investment staff based in the field increased from 256 to 501, with the proportion of field-based to headquarters-based investment staff increasing from 13 percent to 39 percent.

3. See Kaplan and Norton 2001; and Kaplan 2004.

4. From an average of about 43 weeks, according to the 2006 IFC Client Survey.

5. In 2005, average private credit/GDP in high-income countries was 167 percent, similar to the 1996–2005 period average of 169 percent. Source: World Bank Group, Global Development Finance database.

6. Despite representing over 4 percent of global GDP, Latin America has less than 2 percent of the world's total financial assets. See McKinsey & Company 2006, p. 11. Weak banking sector depth is especially noticeable in Argentina, with 11.7 percent in private sector credit/GDP in 2005; Paraguay, with 15.6 percent in private sector credit/GDP in 2005; and Mexico, with 17.9 percent in private sector credit/GDP in 2005. Source: World Bank Group, Global Development Finance database.

7. See IEG-WB 2006a.

8. Derived from World Bank Group, Global Development Finance database.

9. In nonfrontier MICs, the average cost of exporting one container overseas is $1,100, compared with $1,450 per container in frontier countries. Source: Derived from the World Bank Group's *Doing Business* database indicators.

10. Shortcomings in Brazil's port capacity in the early 1990s (referred to in box 2.1) is a case in point. See Farrell, Puron, and Remes 2005, on the need for a strong enabling infrastructure and an effective regulatory structure in helping MICs exploit their comparative advantages.

11. Informal economy output (as a percentage of gross national income) in nonfrontier MICs averages 30 percent. This is not dissimilar to the frontier average of 38 percent. By contrast, the informal economy output in high-income countries is only 17 percent. For a case study on the dampening effects of the informal economy on growth in a MIC, see Elstrodt, Fergie, and Laboissiere 2006.

12. This contrasts with IFC's experience in low-income countries, where development success was 15 percent with a low role and contribution, and 66 percent with a high role and contribution.

13. Excluding China, which accounts for just over 20 percent of developing country GDP and 5 percent of IFC financial sector commitments.

14. IEG-IFC forthcoming(c).

15. See IEG-WB 2006b, 2006c.

16. See IEG-IFC forthcoming(a).

17. The *Africa Action Plan*, approved in September 2005, includes, for example, targets to reduce the costs of business and increase finance mobilization in the region in at least nine countries by fiscal year 2008.

18. IEG-WB 2006a.

19. See IEG-IFC 2005a.

20. From a 2006 XPSR evaluation note. See also IEG-IFC forthcoming(c).

21. See IEG-IFC forthcoming(b).

22. Remittances are today a major component of international financial flows to developing countries, and in the last 10 years they have grown faster than private capital flows or overseas development assistance. Remittances grew more than 300 percent between 1995 and 2005, compared with a 250 percent increase in private capital flows (see World Bank 2006, p. 88).

23. See IEG-IFC 2006a.

24. For example, a business school and a clinic geared toward tourists.

25. See World Bank 2007.

26. World Bank and IFC 2006.

27. See IEG-WB 2006c.

28. *Cooperation* is defined broadly to include any interaction among World Bank Group institutions aimed at improving the development impact of World Bank Group instruments by maximizing synergies and reducing duplication and inconsistencies. It includes both *coordination* (efforts to integrate the strategies of the two institutions to accomplish common objectives, such as through division of labor, but which does not necessarily involve interaction on specific interventions) and *collaboration* (defined as interaction between the two institutions on specific interventions).

29. IEG's evaluation, *Improving Investment Climates: An Evaluation of World Bank Group Assistance* (IEG 2006), reinforces these findings. It concludes that Bank Group coordination on business climate issues has been weak, both within the Bank as well as between the Bank and IFC. Furthermore, the study found that cooperation across the two institutions often depends on personal relationships and the level of attention given to cooperation by senior management.

30. In March 2007, IFC announced new procedures for linking up IFC and Bank advisory services, including: (i) inviting representatives from other parts of the Bank Group to key strategy-setting meetings, where advisory services interventions requiring coordination are discussed, for example, at the regional and sector level; (ii) requesting that task managers seek input/advice from Bank colleagues at the conceptual stage of a project; (iii) sharing information about IFC's portfolio of advisory services operations; and (iv) reimbursement of time-costs associated with the use of Bank staff expertise.

31. Supervision quality was significantly above the average for other regions during 2003–05.

32. Between 2001 and 2006, IFC commitment in South Asia increased by 51 percent, whereas they increased by 106 percent in other regions. Regulatory constraints in India were reportedly a factor in constraining the level of overall investment activity in the region.

33. IEG-IFC's forthcoming report on Ukraine contains a comparison between IFC and EBRD activities in that country in greater detail.

34. From previous annual reviews and reports by IEG-IFC.

35. IEG-WB 2003.

36. More activities are focused on providing access to knowledge and expertise than on ensuring that knowledge is shared in ways that promote its *adaptation and use,* for example, by enhancing active team-based knowledge sharing. Also, activities have done more to *push out* knowledge than to *pull it in*—thereby missing opportunities to refresh the Bank's knowledge through ongoing field experience, to reduce "reinvention of the wheel," and to scale up successful programs. As a result, internal knowledge-sharing activities are not sufficiently relevant to the day-to-day operational work of "frontline" staff.

37. IEG-IFC 2006a.

38. IFC's most recent strategy paper (IFC 2007) sets out a number of risk-management steps IFC is going to take to improve client service and efficiency. These include an ongoing business process review, to both streamline and strengthen operational procedures; a shift in credit review (and, eventually, most aspects of risk-management decision making) to the field; integration of development-impact metrics with financial risk-return metrics, and enhanced tools, such as improved risk-rating systems.

39. The development of new risk-mitigation products is in line with a World Economic Forum recommendation in 2006 that development finance institutions such as IFC expand their risk-mitigation activities. See World Economic Forum 2006, pp. 13–16.

40. See IEG-IFC 2006b.

REFERENCES

EBRD (European Bank for Reconstruction and Development). Projects database. http://www .ebrd.com/projects/eval/method.htm (evaluation methodology and ratings; accessed December 2006).

Elstrodt, Heinz-Peter, Jorge A. Fergie, and Martha A. Laboissiere. 2006. "How Brazil Can Grow." *McKinsey Quarterly* 2: 12–15.

Farrell, Diana, Antonio Puron, and Jaana K. Remes. 2005. "Beyond Cheap Labor: Lessons for Developing Economies." *McKinsey Quarterly* 1: 98–109.

IEG (Independent Evaluation Group). 2004. *Improving Investment Climates: An Evaluation of World Bank Group Assistance*. http://www .worldbank.org/ieg/investment_climates.

———. 2006. *Improving Investment Climates: An Evaluation of World Bank Group Assistance*. Washington, DC: World Bank.

IEG-IFC (Independent Evaluation Group–International Finance Corporation). 2005a. "Food & Agribusiness: An Evaluation of IFC's Investments in the Sector." *IEG Findings*, No. 1, World Bank, Washington, DC.

———. 2005b. "Pakistan: IFC Country Impact Review." *IEG Findings*, No. 3, World Bank, Washington, DC.

———. 2006a. "Annual Review of FY2005 Evaluation Findings in IFC." *IEG Findings*, No. 6, World Bank, Washington, DC.

———. 2006b. "Turkey: IFC Country Impact Review." *IEG Findings*, No. 4, World Bank, Washington, DC.

———. 2007. "IFC's Experience in the Transport Sector." *IEG Evaluation Brief*, No. 8, World Bank, Washington, DC.

———. Forthcoming(a). *Evaluation of IFC's Private Enterprise Partnership Technical Assistance Program in Eastern Europe and Central Asia*. Washington, DC: World Bank.

———. Forthcoming(b). *Evaluation of the Effectiveness of IFC Assistance for the Environment*. Washington, DC: World Bank.

———. Forthcoming(c). *Financing Micro, Small, and Medium Enterprises in Frontier Countries through Financial Intermediaries: An Independent Evaluation of IFC's Experience*. Washington, DC: World Bank.

———. Forthcoming(d). *Ukraine: IFC Country Impact Review*. Washington, DC: World Bank.

IEG-WB (Independent Evaluation Group–World Bank). 2003. *Sharing Knowledge: Innovations and Remaining Challenges*. Washington, DC: World Bank.

———. 2006a. *Annual Review of Development Effectiveness 2006: Getting Results*. Washington, DC: World Bank.

———. 2006b. *Malawi: Country Assistance Evaluation*. Washington, DC: World Bank.

———. 2006c. *Senegal: Country Assistance Evaluation*. Washington, DC: World Bank.

IFC (International Finance Corporation). 2005. "Second Benchmarking Review of ECG Members' Evaluation Practices for Their Private Sector Investment Operations Against Their Agreed Good Practice Standards," by Walter I. Cohn & Associates. Consultant report. http:// www.ifc.org/ifcext/ieg.nsf/AttachmentsByTitle/ Second+Benchmarking+Review+1.25.05_FIN AL/ $FILE/Second+Benchmarking+Review+ 1.25.05_FINAL.pdf.

———. 2006a. *Annual Portfolio Performance Report: FY06*. http://www.ifc.org/ifcext/disclosure .nsf/Content/Annual_Portfolio_Performance_ Review_FY06.

———. 2006b. "IFC Strategic Directions: Implementation Update and FY07–FY09 Outlook." http://www.ifc.org/ifcext/about.nsf/Attachments ByTitle/Strategy_Dev_Paper_2006/$FILE/ Strategy_Dev_Paper_2006.pdf.

———. 2007. "IFC Strategic Directions, FY08–10: Creating Opportunity." Washington, DC. http:// www.ifc.org/ifcext/disclosure.nsf/AttachmentsBy Title/IFC_SDP_full/$FILE/IFC_SDP_full.pdf.

Kaplan, Robert S. 2004. *Strategy Maps: Converting Intangible Assets into Tangible Outcomes.* Boston: Harvard Business School Press.

Kaplan, Robert S., and David P. Norton. 2001. *The Strategy-Focused Organization: How Balanced Scorecard Companies Thrive in the New Business Environment.* Boston: Harvard Business School Press.

McKinsey & Company. 2006. "Mapping the Global Capital Market: Second Annual Report." McKinsey Global Institute. http://www.mckinsey .com/mgi/publications/gcmAnnualReport.asp.

World Bank. 2005. *Meeting the Challenge of Africa's Development: A World Bank Group Action Plan.* Africa Region. Washington, DC, September. http://siteresources.worldbank.org/ EXTAFRREGINICOO/Resources/aap_final.pdf.

———. 2006. *Global Economic Prospects 2006: Economic Implications of Remittances and Migration.* Washington, DC: World Bank.

———. 2007. *Accelerating Development Outcomes in Africa: Progress and Change in the Africa Action Plan.* Africa Region. http:// siteresources.worldbank.org/DEVCOMMINT/ Documentation/21289631/DC2007-0008(E)- AfricaActionPlan.pdf.

———. Forthcoming. *Global Development Finance 2007: Financial Globalization of the Corporate Sector.* Washington, DC: World Bank.

World Bank and IFC. 2006. *Doing Business 2007: How to Reform.* Washington, DC: World Bank.

World Bank Group. Doing Business database. http://www.doingbusiness.org (doing business indicators; accessed December 2006).

———. GDF Online database. http://publications .worldbank.org/GDF (global development finance data; accessed January 2007).

World Economic Forum. 2006. *Building on the Monterrey Consensus: The Untapped Potential of Development Finance Institutions to Catalyze Private Investment.* Geneva: World Economic Forum.